A compilation of
Christmas Stories
from the pages of
the Deseret News

Illustrations by
Robert Noyce
and
Christie Jackson

Deseret News Publishing Company
Salt Lake City, Utah

Christmas I Remember Best, Copyright ©1983 by the Deseret News Publishing Co. All rights reserved. Printed in the United States of America. No part of this book may be used or reproduced in any manner whatsoever without written permission of the Deseret News Publishing Company, except in the case of brief quotations embodied in critical articles and reviews. For information write the Deseret News, 30 East First South Street, P.O. Box 1257, Salt Lake City, Utah 84110.

ISBN 0-910901-00-7

Table of contents

The bon-bon bomber   1
   By Gail Halvorsen (1976)
A proud woman's love   5
   By Kathleen Forgie (1979)
Our blessed Christmas   9
   By Drucilla H. McFarland (1972)
There is a way   13
   By Jay Hess (1975)
The king of hearts   17
   By Max B. Richardson (1981)
Santa wore a badge   21
   By Capt. Owen Poulson (1958)

A gift for Louise *By Mrs. Pearl B. Mason (1962)*	23
Christmas for Earl *By Tom Davenport (1974)*	27
Santa in a brown Chevy *By Jeanne Anthony (1980)*	31
Man with the camera *By Kathleen Chipman (1979)*	35
Honesty's reward *By Thomas J. Griffiths (1975)*	39
Sharing Christmas *By Terri Lynn Johnson (1981)*	43
A Christmas friend *By Connie Wilcox (1981)*	47
A greater power *By Kenneth J. Brown (1960)*	51
A hair-raising tale *By Peggy M. Cook (1977)*	55
Playing Santa Claus *By Rhea Hart Grandy (1979)*	59
Santa Claus boycotted *By Dorothy See (1978)*	63
Bear was there, too! *By Mrs. Farren Keyte (1971)*	67
Mike in the nick of time *By Mrs. Erna Park (1961)*	71
Christmas spirit takes time *By Alan DeMann (1977)*	73
Ray of hope *By Bernice Brown (1962)*	77
Will no one help? *By Jacqueline Frushour (1977)*	81
A star of the past *By John B. Matheson, Jr. (1964)*	85

A gift from Jimmy   87
    By Jettie J. Anderson (1964)
A chocolate Christmas   91
    By Richard R. Schaar (1961)
Mrs. T's potbelly   93
    By Mrs. Alma C. Nielsen (1974)
Only a small part in the Christmas play   97
    By Mavis H. Steadman (1981)
Christmas dolls   101
    By Beatrice Toman Gardner (1960)
A gift of friendship   105
    By LaRue H. Soelberg (1970)
A surprise visitor   109
    By Erin Parsons (1982)
When out on the lawn . . .   113
    By Ramona Stover (1959)
A gift of Christmas   115
    By Mrs. W. R. Swinyard (1971)
Boxes full of love   119
    By Hope M. Williams (1959)
Wartime Christmas   123
    By Mrs. Sije Terpstra (1959)
Dreams go up in smoke   127
    By Richard Menzies (1979)
My unloved doll   131
    By Annie Atkin Tanner (1961)
Silent Night in the wind   135
    By Rheauma West (1972)
A timeless Christmas   139
    By Ferenc Molnar (1976)
The Spirit of Christmas   143
    By Arnold E. Brady (1962)
Freckle cream Christmas   147
    By J. Stanford Staheli (1982)

Foreword

Memories. What is Christmas without them? From the universal memory of that first Great Gift, to the half-remembered Santa Claus-waiting excitement of earliest childhood, to the glow of last year's lights on Temple Square, Christmas is memories.

For 25 years, the Deseret News has shared the memories of its readers through its annual "Christmas I Remember Best" feature. Compiled here for the first time are stories representative of the many hundreds—more than 500 the first year alone— submitted by readers over the past quarter century.

Reading them reemphasizes some simple truths well-known, too little understood. Like:

Christmases that count, that are remembered, center on people, not things.

They involve giving, not getting.

They revolve around people in difficult, not prosperous, circumstances. The beauty of a child with two months to live; the Christmas Eve loss of a father's only $10 bill; the Christmas Day spent by ordinary people not enjoying their gifts and feasting but cleaning up a neighbor's burned-out store; the effort to create Christmas in the bitterness of a North Vietnam prison camp—these are the stuff of which memorable Christmases are made. These, and the birth of a baby boy in a strange, friendless city among despot-ridden people.

There's another thread that runs through these stories, most of them. They are written by women. And why not? Women give heart to Christmas. They feel it. They are the sensitive ones with a special sense of needs and meanings and promise. It is they, mostly, who remember. As did another women, who "kept all these things, and pondered them in her heart."

The memories of Christmas. May yours be as meaningful to you and yours.

William B. Smart
Editor and General Manager
Deseret News Publishing Company
September 1, 1983

The bon-bon bomber

By Gail Halvorsen

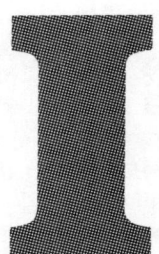 WILL NEVER FORGET the Christmas I had over — not in — Berlin in 1948. Only a year before I could never had imagined I'd spend December shuttling 6,500 pounds of lollipops, candy bars and gobs of gum under armed guard to a jail cell for safekeeping. Even now it is hard to believe it all really happened.

I was a lieutenant in the Air Force, and a pilot when I volunteered to fly in food and fuel shortly after the Berlin Airlift began in 1948.

The West Berliners, our avowed enemies during World War II, were asking our help to preserve their freedom. They had been cut off from all land supplies by Russian troops.

At first I thought we'd only be there for a short time, that world opinion wouldn't allow the Russians to try to starve two and a half million people for that long. I didn't think the world would stand for blatant disrespect for human dignity.

Because a plane landed in Berlin with supplies every few minutes, there was no time to see the city. After my last flight one day, I hitched a ride back to Berlin on another plane, determined to use my "sleep time" to see the city.

Movie camera in hand, I walked two and a half miles from the landing point to the edge of Tempelhof Airport expecting to take movies of the planes landing and departing.

I noticed a silent group of about 30 German children standing next to the barbed wire watching me. They were pale and quiet, their clothes patched in many places. I knew they had barely enough to eat.

The children began speaking to me in pretty good English, and, after an hour of this I had to leave.

I walked about 50 yards before it struck me that these children had not asked me for anything. You see, everywhere else I had been — Africa, Great Britain, South America — the children figured an American was a soft touch. They'd all crowd around and say things like, "Any gum, chum?" or "Any bon-bon?" But these children were different, they didn't ask for anything.

So I reached into my pocket and was embarrassed that I only had two sticks of gum.

However, I broke them in two and gave them to the children in the front. I couldn't believe the grateful expression on all their faces. They didn't rush, or push or shove, which I marveled at. The four who had taken the gum unwrapped the tiny pieces carefully and passed the paper around — the other children had sheer delight on their faces just to smell the wrappers.

An idea struck me. With only 30 cents, I could get a piece of gum for each of them. But how could I get it to them? I wouldn't likely have time to visit again.

So I told them to stand in a clearing near the airport to catch little parachutes with candy tied to them that I'd drop.

"How will we know which plane is you?" they asked.

I told them I'd come by the next day and wiggle my wings back and forth when I sighted them. (When I was learning how to fly out of Brigham City, I used to go over dad's beet field and say "Hi" to him that way.)

So, I put together some candy bars and gum in three little handkerchief parachutes, saw the children and dropped the candy through the flare chute behind the pilot's seat.

I was absolutely not going to drop any more after the first time. But other buddies in my squadron said they kept seeing a group of children looking up from the ground waving at them — as if they expected something. So I kept it up.

You see, what I was doing was against regulations and I was known as a stickler for going by the book. It was only a few weeks before I was "caught" and called in by the commander.

He said he had planned to chew me out but the general had called and congratulated the squadron for such a novel goodwill gesture.

A story about this candy bombing we were doing hit the German headlines when one of my chutes nearly struck a German reporter on the head. After the article was repeated all across America, I started getting massive amounts of candy and handkerchiefs for the squad's "sweet" flights. You must remember that this candy was in addition to the food and coal we were airlifting.

Soon I began getting letters from grateful Berlin children addressed to "Uncle Wiggly Wings," "The Bon-Bon Bomber," "The Raisin Bombadier," and even "Schokoladenflleger."

I received one letter that had a beautiful map with it. The little girl said hers was the white house with chickens in the backyard and that she would be waiting there at 2 p.m. I never found her house so I mailed her some candy.

I even received letters from children in East Berlin who said they "didn't like Russians either, please drop some candy to us."

I'd estimate that by December, 90,000 miniature candy chutes had fluttered down into various parts of Berlin. It had become a massive operation that we dubbed "Operation Little Vittles" since the Berlin Airlift itself was "Operation Vittles."

With Christmas coming, my buddies and I wanted to do something special.

So when I went back to the U.S. for a brief visit in the fall I met with the president of the American Confectionaires Association who pledged he'd send me some boxes of candy.

During the first week of December a West German military policeman called and said he was forwarding a railroad car with 3,000 pounds of candy to the Rhein-Main air base!

It wasn't long before a second shipment of 3,500 pounds came in. The sum included contributions from the association and cities all over the U.S. — including a sizable amount from my hometown of Garland, Box Elder County.

The 6,500 pounds of candy was too much to drop but we knew we would get it to the children.

I contacted American authorities in Berlin who were setting up Christmas parties all over West Berlin. I told them I'd furnish dessert for the parties. The American Air Force colonel could hardly talk, "Gee," he said, "as bad off as they are that would be great."

We boxed all of the candy and flew in 100 pounds each trip to Tempelhof. An officer would greet the plane and take the boxes to the Berlin jail where they steadily filled up two cells with the sweets.

The security was necessary because of the extreme black market value of the candy. For two candy bars, a West German lady did my laundry each week. At one Christmas show, Americans offered a stick of gum to each child who would come to the 1,800 seat theater. Some 3,500 children had to be turned away.

By December 23, all the candy was in Berlin being distributed to the party sites.

The parties began mid-afternoon December 24th, since the children had to be home by dark. West Berlin was under a mandatory blackout each night.

Myself? At first I thought it was unfair when I had to fly Christmas Eve. But it gave me time to think.

As I left the West German base for the last of my 450-mile round trips that night, fireworks exploded around me. But in West Berlin there was only darkness. On Christmas Eve, it was eerie.

What a people! I thought. Surrounded as they were, an island in an ocean of Russian troops, they fought on, living on half-rations. Just weeks before, during a general election, 99 out of 100 West Berliners had voted dramatically against acceptance of Communism.

How could I be anything but grateful for having known these people?

Some four dozen U.S. and British airmen died during the airlift in plane crashes and other accidents. Only two weeks after Christmas, when the airlift was 200 days old, shabbily-dressed Berliners brought modest gifts to the fliers at the airport, often breaking through informal police cordons to personally give their presents.

For me, Christmas 1948 had few of the little trinkets and symbols normally associated with that season. But I had learned what freedom was. I had memories enough for a lifetime and a joy it is difficult to describe. All for two sticks of gum.

A proud woman's love
By Kathleen Forgie

AS THE YEARS PASS and Christmases fade into one collective, undistinguishable blur, it's hard to remember who gave what on which Dec. 25. The gifts were always fine, the trees always crisps-scented and beautiful, the memories always repetitively organized in photo albums.

But Christmas 1959 was special. I was 12 then. Most of the previous sumemr and early fall I spent across the street at Mary Von der Rijn's house. She was older than I, maybe 15, but those were the years of self-awareness when looking and "being" older than you were seemed important. So I hung around with Mary.

Mary's family was different. Her mother was about the right age, but her father was over 80. He sat on their front porch when the weather was warm, a white, shrunken figure in a wide brimmed hat and black glasses that identified him as blind.

In back of their house in a converted garage lived an old woman, tall but bent, her hair still mostly black and always pulled back from her thinly rugged face in a pioneer fashion. She was a woman no one in Mary's household talked about except to say she was the first Mrs. Von der Rijn.

The Old Woman didn't leave her house often. Occasionally, she would pad to the store for groceries, steadying herself with a cane and sometimes pulling a three-wheeled cart behind her, always looking at the ground. Her figure was old, tired.

There was something majestic about that Old Woman and intimidating, like most "objects" of neighborhood curiosity. She was intensely proud and doggedly independent as I soon learned. And bitter.

We met accidently on a Saturday in late October. The morning was crackling clear but cold, and as I made the familiar trek across the street, ungloved hands shoved in coat pockets, I thought how good it would feel to be indoors again.

When I entered Mary's yard and headed toward the back door, I spotted the Old Woman. She was stooped over, gathering wood from a large pile next to her house, her large sweater buttoned from hip to chin against the frost. I hesitated only for a moment, swallowed my timidity and walking toward her, offered my help.

She peered through deep-set, cataract-clouded eyes, smiled crookedly and accepted my offer. "But," she added emphatically, "I want to pay you." I declined, but she insisted. She carried two pieces of wood to her door moving in hobbled but quick steps, her cane marking the way. I chose four or five pieces of pine, deposited them on her doorstep and went back for kindling when the Old Woman approached, breathless but elated.

She uncurled her long fingers and placed a coin in my hand. "I want you to take this quarter," she said and then asked, "It is a quarter, isn't it? My eyes are not too good anymore." I assured her she had given me the proper amount, thanked her and together we walked the short distance to her door.

The Old Woman didn't invite me in, so I stacked the wood in her arms and held the screen door open. She walked down the skinny, dark kitchen to a black wood stove and very slowly stretched over a box, releasing the wood. She came back for the kindling, said thank you and goodbye.

I put the nickel she had given me in my pocket and headed for home, deciding not to visit Mary.

That was the beginning of a distant, but oddly warm relationship. I continued to help her carry wood that fall and she always paid me — sometimes a quarter, sometimes a nickel, but she never invited me in.

The week before Christmas, I took $10 in baby-sitting money down to Sprouse-Reitz to shop for my family; ten dollars went a long way twenty years ago, especially at a five and dime. I had nine people on my Christmas list that year — my parents, my brother, two aunts, two grandmothers, a grandfather and a girlfriend. That worked out to about a dollar apiece with some left over to buy a sundae at the pharmacy up the street.

On my way to the checkout counter, I passed a stack of aprons and thought of the Old Woman. She always wore a bib apron over her dress, under the baggy gray sweater. I searched the pile and finally decided on a bright, blue-flowered one, neatly bordered in bias tape and trimmed on the large pockets with blue rickrack. It was 49 cents, the price of a chocolate sundae.

The day before Christmas, I delivered her present. The Old Woman didn't answer my knock for several minutes and when she did, she clutched her sweater close, blocking the snowy chill. She looked weary.

"Merry Christmas," I said and pushed the present toward her. The Old Woman looked first at the gift and then at me. Her cloudy eyes misted and she beamed a full-faced, cheek-to-cheek smile. Then she invited me in.

The visit was short and when I left, I was humming soundlessly, breathing in great chunks of winter air and feeling Christmas.

It was mid-morning on Dec. 25 when the Old Woman knocked on our door. She was wearing galoshes, heavy stockings, a scarf, her tightly buttoned sweater and my apron. She would come in, but instead handed me a small white box tied with twine. "This is for you," she smiled, "for what you've done. Merry Christmas."

In almost the same breath as my "Thank You," the Old Woman turned and refusing aid, carefully paced the three steps from our porch. Without looking back, she walked away.

I closed the door, sat down and stared at the unadorned, rectangular box. "To Cathy" was penciled shakily across the top. I pulled the string, opened the lid and choked. Inside was a small bottle of Jergens' lotion, a bar of Ivory soap, a plain Hershey's chocolate bar and a package of gum, spearmint.

At that moment, all the presents under the tree, so many of them were non-existent. Christmas was there, in that small paper box.

Winter passed quietly and with warming weather, my visits tapered and eventually stopped. Then one day after the last snows melted, after the bottle of Jergens was empty and the Ivory soap used up, I saw the Old Woman in my freshly starched blue apron hobble to the store. I waved, but she didn't see me. The next day I learned she had died in her sleep. ❄

Our blessed Christmas

By Mrs. Drucilla H. McFarland

IT MUST HAVE BEEN a long time that we had been ill. My sister Eleanor and I were in the same bed. Across the room were Stella and Bea. Out in the large living room I could see Joe and Will in a bed on the floor. They were only staying in it occasionally, meantime slipping around to tease us girls.

Sadie, the eldest, was up and about now and helping mother.

"It's just like you children to all come down at once with measles. Then Joe gets out for one day and comes back with chicken pox to start all around the circle again," Ma complained good naturedly. She took the tin wash basin from Bea and handed her a towel and comb and then stopped before Stella. Joe slipped behind her and put one of Pinkie's new kittens on top of her head, nearly causing the upset of the water.

"Young man," Ma scolded, "would you like a taste of thimble pie for your breakfast this morning (a rap with a thimbled finger)?"

"I'd like anything, Ma, that's different from flummity."

Bea wailed. "Are we going to have that brown flour mush again?"

Ma's eyes filled with tears and she turned quickly to put another stick into the round pot-bellied iron stove.

"Tomorrow is Christmas," Joe said, "I'll bet if Pa was here. . ."

"Where is Pa?" little Eleanor queried. Sadie put her arms around Eleanor, looking very sad, too, since Ma had gone outside and closed the door softly to cry all by herself.

"Ellie," Sadie said to this little sister. "Pa has just gone on another mission."

"That's what Ma says, but it has been so long."

"Longer even than last time," Bea said. She was hardly old enough to realize that this mission would be endless. She remembered and wanted the joyousness of his last return from the church mission in Tennessee. She wanted to forget how the neighbor children hurt her by telling her, "Forget the mission story. Your father got killed building the Weber bridge."

Mother, coming back in, asked Will if he thought he could walk to the big hill and cut a cedar for our Christmas tree. Of course he could.

She brought popcorn she had raised and set Joe to preparing it for the girls to make strands of decorations, with the understanding that we did not eat too much of it.

Our meal of flummity and milk was just finished the next morning when we heard sleigh bells. Joe pulled back the curtain that mother kept over the window to protect our measle-sore eyes from the light. "Ma, it's a man with a sleigh load of. . ."

Mother answered the knock at our door and the man walked in carrying a shank of beef.

Before she could frame her speech of rejection he said, "No use to say no, Sister Holmes. This is my privilege of having a happy Christmas by giving one."

Our mother knew that this good man believed every word he spoke. He was William McFarland. His Scotch father's family and her Scotch father John Martin were close neighbors in pioneering the new town of West Weber.

"But I have no money to pay," Mother said.

"Sister Holmes, that's the reason I am here. Just enjoying my privilege of helping the widows and the fatherless."

"But I have never accepted charity from anyone before."

"That I know, too, and my wish is that you need not again. But now, Merry Christmas and may God bless you all!"

We could think of roast, gravy, suet pudding!

Ma got out the skillet while Joe whittled thin chips from the frozen round and we sat down to our second breakfast that morning. Mother said, "William, you ask the blessing."

Will, just coming sixteen, was the man of the house now and he could offer a proper prayer of thanks. He said the words aloud and everyone of us repeated them in our hearts: "We thank Thee Heavenly Father for this blessed Christmas Day."

'There is a Way'

By Jay Hess

'IS THERE ROOM FOR ONE MORE in there.'

A casually dressed, nearly all-American air force pilot carefully picked his way around and over the slightly boisterous crowd seated on the floor. The last space was not filled.

On a screen in the Tahkli, Thailand, officers' club flashes the story of the men who fly the F105 over North Vietnam. The title: "There is a Way."

An hour before, the late comer was in a sweat-stained flight suit, debriefing his flight over the north. There has been lots of flak, some MIGs and SAMs. A faint voice caught his ear. It came from someone behind him. The voice said, kiddingly, "There ain't no way." It has been a close call.

Three months passed. Our latecomer, now looking anything but all-American, awaits Christmas 1967 in a Hanoi prison. He is with three newly made friends. There is no use even thinking or talking about the Christmas Spirit. "There ain't no way."

Christmas Eve comes. Our despondent former fliers feel a little moved by the Spirit of Christmas as the camp radio, in poorest fidelity, plays Christmas music, to everyone's astonishment.

Later, the peep hatch on the door opens.

A small package, from the minister of the Evangelical Church of the DRVN, is handed in. It contains four small plastic bags, each with a tangerine, a cookie and a few pieces of candy. A couple of POWs feel bad for not doing more to promote the Spirit of Christmas.

As usual, on Christmas morning, as on every other morning throughout the year, the camp gong rings. The four sleep in, taking advantage of the Christmas Spirit. They are later startled awake by the sound of keys and a bang on the door. They scramble to their feet. Two of the four stumble around looking for a missing rubber tire sandal.

"Better hurry, the turnkey is coming in," the other two whisper in unison.

With one shoe off and one shoe on, they start toward the door. Then they stop in amazement. There, across the room, is a Christmas tree. Santa's been there!

For an instant, through sleepy eyes and in the confusion, it is real — a real Christmas tree. And no one could get in there — except Santa.

The guards yell. We line up. Then the spell is broken — like Cinderella's coach at midnight.

The Christmas tree is just a tea pot with a small broom placed in it handle down. Wrapped around it for tinsel is gauze from a bandage. Stuck between the straws are a few candy wrappers for balls. Scattered beneath are a few tangerine peelings and fallen leaves which had been carefully gathered from the courtyard over the previous days. And there, lined up before the tree, are the two missing sandals. On them had been placed two colorfully-wrapped pieces of candy. I had seen a similar sight in previous years when we were in Germany.

Well, two of us learned a big lesson that day. Even when you think there is not a Way, "There is a Way." So on every Christmas Eve from then on, I hung up my stocking. There was always something good in it Christmas morning.

It helped to keep that lesson in mind. Even then, if someone would have told me that day, "You've got to hang on for five more years," it would have been a great test. The kidding response may have been, "There ain't no Way."

"There was a Way." For it I thank a lot of people.

First, our courageous President, then my family and you who worked to improve our treatment, those who prayed, wrote letters, wore bracelets and all who have written to express their joy at my return.

And thanks to all who have done so much for us since we've come home.

On Christmas, try to remember with me, "There is a Way."

The king of hearts

By Max B. Richardson

HE FRONT DOOR OF THE Calico Cat Saloon burst open and in a flurry of snowflakes a small boy darted in. It was Christmas Eve and the Calico Cat Saloon was hardly the place you would expect to find such a small lad; but there he was, wet and shivering cold. He was a skinny tow-headed kid, only 9 or 10 years and there was a wistful, almost sad look in his eyes. In place of a coat he wore a threadbare sweater over his patched pair of striped bib overalls; and his feet were clad only in worn-out canvas gym shoes that were soaking wet and made a squishing sound with each step he took.

The boy's eyes scanned the smoke-filled room. Then he ran squishing past the bar toward the rear of the room where men sat huddled around a large round table that was covered with green felt.

"Daddy, mama sent me to get you!" the boy exclaimed, smiling with delight in having found his father.

"I'm not ready to go home yet, boy," his father said, without looking up from his cards.

My father, Lewis Hillman Richardson, sat in the dealer's chair that snowy Christmas Eve. Compared to Pa most card sharks were little more than toothless minnows. There were not laws out west in those days to restrict such things; and I guess he figured that for a man with only a fifth grade education, dealing cards was a lot easier that digging ditches or most other things he might have done for a living.

I had only stopped in to wish Dad a Merry Christmas, but with the appearance of this tiny waif, I couldn't resist staying longer. Would he get his father home before he lost all of his paycheck? How would my dad react to this little stranger? I knew he thought amateurs who gambled with professionals were fools. Losing their money was a just reward for their stupidity, but what about the tiny boy and his brothers and sisters? What was their reward to be?

Dad was a large rugged man who looked the part of the gambler he was; but I knew something about the tough old gambler that others didn't know — underneath that rough, calloused exterior beat the tender heart of a sentimental old softie.

"Come on, daddy," pleaded the boy, after his father lost again. "We won't have grocery money."

"You'd better take that boy home before he catches pneumonia," said my father.

"I'll worry about him," snapped the man. "You worry about your dealing!" The boy's father continued to lose heavily.

"Please come home, daddy," sobbed the boy.

"Just one more hand," the man said, still never looking at his son; a phrase he was to repeat again and again as long as his money would last. Finally he had lost it all. He hadn't had much money to start with, only 40 or 50 dollars. But 40 or 50 dollars is a lot of money when it's all you've got, and it was all he had.

"I told you you'd lose it all, daddy!" the boy sobbed. The boy's father got up without a word and walked toward the door, the boy at his heels, still sobbing.

"That's all for tonight," Dad said, as he got up from the table. Some of the men who wanted to gamble longer grumbled. "It's Christmas Eve and I'm going to spend what's left of it with my family," Dad snapped. He scooped up the night's winnings and gave the money to old Vick, the owner of the saloon. "Here, count this and give me what I've got coming," he said.

My father hurried after the man and his little boy, and caught them just before they reached the door. The money the boy's father had lost belonged to the saloon. It was not my father's to give back; but he felt so bad about what had happened that he took 40 dollars of his own money out of his pocket and kneeling on one knee, he tucked it into the little boy's pocket.

"Merry Christmas, lad," Pa said with an affectionate smile. "Now take your daddy home."

"Big night, Lewie," said Vick, handing Dad his pay.

"Yes, the suckers were really biting tonight, Vick; but that was the last game I'll ever deal."

"You make joke, Lewie," said Vick. "You can't mean that."

"I mean it all right — I'm through," Dad said, as we walked toward the door. "Seeing that ragged half-starved little boy tonight made me realize just how bad gambling really is and I'll have no more of it."

"You'll be back, Lewie," old Vick taunted. "You don't know anything but gambling."

"Maybe not, but there's one thing I do know — I don't have to steal food from children to get my daily bread," said Dad as the door closed behind us.

All my life I had lived in the shadow of the town gambler. A stigma seemed to follow my sister and me wherever we went. At school or even at Sunday School it was always the same — we were the town gambler's kids. Nothing could ever change that. But that snowy Christmas Eve at the Calico Cat Saloon, I wouldn't have traded that tough old gambler for the fanciest bank president in town. Nor would I have traded him in the years that followed, for he kept his word. Even though it often meant working dirty knuckle-busting, backbreaking jobs that paid him but a fraction of what he could have earned as a gambler, to the day he died he never touched another card. ❄

Santa wore a badge

By Capt. Owen Poulsen

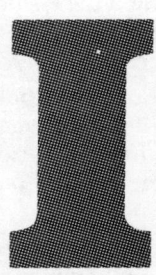IT WAS A BRISK WINTER day in Salt Lake City. The date was Dec. 17, 1927. A thick blanket of snow coverd Utah. Downtown streets were clogged with Christmas shoppers.

Main Street was gaily decorated with colorful evergreen trees which sparkled with glistening snow. The temperature dipped to near zero. Shoppers bundled in warm clothing.

Salt Lake City was full of the Christmas spirit. The University of Utah had just let out for the holidays. Students at West High School rehearsed for their annual Christmas play, titled "Child Jesus."

Volunteers of America and Salvation Army workers tinkled bells on Main Street and collected coins for the poor.

The afternoon edition of the Deseret News reported Utah experienced a "prosperous year" in 1927. But there were still many who faced a scant Christmas.

Mrs. Lillie Rosenkrantz was one such person. She had six

small children to feed and clothe, let alone buy Christmas presents. But she was a resourceful woman and had worked hard for five days doing housework to earn $10 so she could brighten her children's little faces on Christmas morn.

Mrs. Rosenkrantz browsed through downtown stores trying to decide what she would buy for her litle ones. In one department store she stopped to look at some toys on the counter.

"Now, let me see," she thought. "Perhaps this teddy bear would be good for the tiny one."

She motioned to a clerk. "I'll take this," she said, reaching for her purse where she left it on the counter.

Mrs. Rosenkrantz' heart skipped a beat. The purse was gone. Someone had stolen it while she was looking at the teddy bear.

Tears welled in her eyes as she hurried from the store. Five days' pay and a merry Christmas for her little children were whisked away by the adept fingers of a thief.

Outside the store Officer George J. Buckway whistled as he walked his beat down Main Street. He was happy. Christmas was just around the corner and it was pay day. He felt the stiff pay envelope in his overcoat pocket as he walked. With a wife and seven children he had a lot to be thankful for.

His thoughts were interrupted as Mrs. Rosenkrantz, in tears, ran from the department store. It took him five minutes to get the full story from the crying woman.

"We can report this at headquarters," the officer said. "Maybe the money will turn up." But deep down in his heart he knew the money would never be recovered.

On the way back to the station, Officer Buckway thought about Christmas. What kind of Christmas will this woman and her six children have this year? Then he thought of his own children and what it would be like if he lost his pay envelope.

Before they got to the station Officer Buckway stopped. He reached into his pocket and pulled out his pay envelope.

"Here, take this," he said, handing Mrs. Rosenkrantz a crisp $10 bill. "You and your little ones have a merry Christmas."

Mrs. Rosenkrantz' tears of sadness turned to tears of joy. There really is a Santa Claus, she said. He's a big husky cop and he walks a beat on Main Street.

As Officer Buckway went back to his beat there was a warm feeling in his heart. With a cop's pay only $125 a month and with seven hungry children to feed, it would certainly be a scant Christmas in the Buckway home this year, he thought. But he still had lots to be thankful for.

A gift for Louise

By Mrs. Pearl B. Mason

WAS TEACHING FOURTH GRADE in my home town in Wyoming. It was the day before our Christmas program was to be given. School routine was forgotten as we sang carols and rehearsed plays under the magic spell of the lighted Christmas tree. Names were drawn and apparently all the pupils had brought their gifts.

In this class was a girl who was different from the rest of the pupils, because of her almost indescribably unkempt, frowsy appearance. She came from a family of nine healthy, robust, aggressive children. There was none of this in Louise. I never think of her but I picture a frail child standing before me in a long, loose dress, pinned at the neck with a big safety pin, and a sash wound around her waist trying to keep the oversized dress on her tiny frame. Her mousy hair always stood out like cockleburr and she would wait for me every morning at the top of the stairs and stammer, "G-g-good morning," to me. I always responded kindly to her greeting, and her face would light up with a smile that would almost turn her inside out. If Louise had any enthusiasm for anything, it was to find someone who would befriend her.

I had wondered who had drawn Louise's name. Since I had heard nothing, I had supposed everyone had accepted the name he had drawn with kindness and all was well.

As I returned to my room after dismissing the class for the day, I was surprised to find one of the girls waiting beside my desk. She held a small square box in her hand, and quietly she began to tell me her story.

Walter, the most popular boy in the class, had drawn Louise's name and had wrapped a big piece of coal in tissue paper for her. It was easily recognizable under the tree. Hazel was afraid it would make Louise cry. Could she please replace it with this present? She had earned it by helping her father in his general store after school.

Well, the big moment finally arrived. The Christmas program was over and Santa had come in to distribute the presents. No one recognized the janitor behind the genial Santa mask as he began calling names and handing out gifts. I realized that this tree and the gift under it would be all the Christmas little Louise would know. Her eyes were dancing and she could hardly keep her seat for excitement as she listened eagerly for her name to be called.

The boys were excited, too. They knew which name Walter had drawn and they were curious to see what he had done about it. He was anxious, too — to prove to his buddies that he had no affection for the person whose name he had drawn.

Finally Santa called "Louise." She almost climbed over herself to get out of her seat and to claim her present. Each gift so far had been a nice one.

The sound of snickering among the boys stopped and all eyes were on Louise as she was handed the little square box. Nervously she began unwrapping the package. Suddenly a feeling of real joy filled every heart as we saw the wonderful expression of happiness and surprise that came to Louise's face as she lifted her gift from its box.

"A doll," she whispered, cuddling it to her and rocking it tenderly in her arms as she returned to her seat, where she continued to pour out upon it all the love and affection for which she so earnestly yearned.

To Louise the doll was not a gift from anyone — rather a Miracle of the Christmas Tree.

To the rest of us, it was the Miracle of Christmas! A dramatization of the fact that it is blessed to make someone happy. No one had really meant to hurt or be unkind. Hazel, in her remembering "one of the least of these," had made it possible for the true spirit of Christmas to be magnified in every heart that day.

It was as though our little Louise had become the Christ Child before our very eyes.

Christmas for Earl
By Tom Davenport

IT JUST DIDN'T SEEM like the day before Christmas. Was it the weather? The cold, dull-gray sky left no doubt winter had come. But there was no snow to whitewash the dead grass, decaying leaves or broken tree limbs everywhere.

Maybe I was getting too old. At the adult age of fourteen, I had no more fantasies about Santa Claus — and hadn't for years. But I did believe in Christmas.

For my family, there was nothing missing that season. We had followed all the holiday hullaballoo, including the heavily ornamented Christmas tree, traditional fruitcake and Sunday School class caroling and had applauded my high school's annual best-Christmas-play-ever.

But as my best friend, Lyle, and I took a late afternoon walk, kicking cans into the mud while a soft fog settled around us, I couldn't see any sparkle to this Christmas. Was I, actually, too old? Or was it the lack of snow?

Perhaps Dec. 25, 1962, would have passed like all the other Christmases if it hadn't been for a garbage truck and a lonely, 45-year-old bachelor.

Earl was the best thing that ever happened to my friends and me. He lived alone in a treasure-house of tropical fish, racing magazines, games and oil paints. Perhaps it was the unused father in him that prompted Earl to let us use his place as a clubhouse — even when he was gone. Yet somehow he made us feel as if we had adopted him.

Earl had a face which, according to the owner himself, "could stop a bull elephant's charge." The crater-pocked visage (he said it was the result of an ice-pick street fight) was only emphasized by brown, chipped teeth. Earl was tall and bony and sported a scruffy chin beard. Under an old beret he hid hair that was always in a state of suspended indecision — somewhere between crewcut and uncut. Earl's clothes had a moldy, musty odor and his shirt (better said, THE shirt) was an autobiography, revealing his hobbies, occupation and last month's diet.

With no family and, especially, no children of his own, Earl had no use for Christmas. Besides, he often told us bluntly (never bitterly) he didn't believe in Christ. So why celebrate His birthday?

As Lyle and I walked along that afternoon, our talk was mostly about Earl. We knew he'd go to a friend's house for Christmas Eve, but also knew Earl wouldn't do a thing to make December 25th a different day.

It wasn't long before we'd reached the sidewalk's end and saw ahead, through the fog, the figure of a man tossing leftover Christmas trees into a truck parked in the supermarket's dirt lot. An idea struck us both. Even though we ran, we reached the truck just as the driver was pulling away from the curb.

"Hey, mister!" I called to get his attention. "Can we have one of your trees? We want to give it to a friend."

He turned, looked at us for a moment, then answered: "Sure, take one."

We grabbed the nearest tree — small, a bit misshapen, but it was green and fragrant. "Thanks!" I yelled, as the truck lurched away.

"What time is it?" I asked Lyle.

"Five o'clock," he replied. Earl would be gone, leaving the house unlatched, as always, in case we dropped in. It didn't take long to drag the tree to his house, which was open and empty. After a small struggle, Lyle and I finally placed it in the corner of Earl's living room and stood back to gaze on it.

"Tom," Lyle said, with a discouraged look on his face, "What are we going to put on the tree?"

"Don't worry," I answered. "A couple of months ago I was helping Earl put some stuff in the attic. We found a boxful of Christmas decorations that the Bartons had left when they moved. I bet they're still up there."

They were. But the two strings of lights and small assortment of ornaments sent us hurrying home for more. I returned with an old star and some scratched and dented silver balls, since replaced in our home by newer ones. Lyle brought more globes, an assortment of plastic reindeer and angels, a slightly matted string of tinsel and some icicles.

Soon it was finished. Excitedly we turned off the lights and switched on the tree. The room was filled with the soft, glowing magic of Christmas, accented by the pine needles' rich fragrance. We both stood silently.

Lyle broke the silence. "What about presents?" he asked. "The stores are all closed — what can we get him?"

I thought for a moment.

"Why don't we go around the neighborhood and see if they can donate something for Earl?" I suggested.

So we did. The Claytons gave us some oranges, and a package of hard candy. The Hogans donated a loaf of banana bread. Mr. Hall had a carton of .22 shells he gave up. Mom offered a fruitcake and some frosted Christmas cookies. After the Johns added a box of cherry chocolates, we busied ourselves wrapping the offerings and putting them under the tree. Taking a sock from one of Earl's drawers, we filled it with food and, since he had no fireplace, taped it to the arm of his couch.

It was finished. The tree was misshapen and the decorations old and shoddy, yet it has to be the most beautiful tree I had seen then — or since!

It was late, and time to go. I took one last look to memorize the sight, trying to imagine the look of Earl's face when he saw it. Then we left through the front door, shutting it tightly behind us.

As I stepped out into the darkness, a gentle moistness caressed my face.

"Look, Tom, it's snowing!" Lyle exclaimed.

Sure enough, it was. Large, heavy flakes were falling through the moonlit fog. It had just begun, only a light fluff covered the ground.

Lyle ran and jumped in front of me, whooping for joy. "Yahoo!" he cried. "Christmas has come at last!"

And it had.

As I gazed into the tumbling whiteness, I was filled with a strange, warm, inner peace that for years I had associated with Christmas. I guess I wasn't getting too old. Or was it the snow? ❄

Santa in a brown Chevy

By Jeanne Anthony

HE GHOST OF CHRISTMAS PAST sweeps up the torn tinsel and wrapping paper of another yuletide. There is a comfortable sameness about the holiday season most year. But once in a while something different happens that sets the memory of one Christmas apart from all others forever. Such was the Christmas of 1964.

The holidays were over and the school where I was a speech therapist was back in session. At 11:00 the third period group came in. They were all boys, six of them. When they opened the door and came in, it was as if someone had spilled a bag of marbles into my tiny room. They alternately bumped into each other, then scattered every which way. Finally they were all gathered up and seated in a semi-circle around my chair.

Frankie Wilson came in last. Taking care not to cause trouble, he shyly took a chair at the end of the curved row, a little apart from the others. Before he sat down, he tugged at the too-short legs of his trousers, in a vain attempt to make them closer to his feet. The elastic was gone from his socks and they lay in folds around the bottoms of his ankles, except at the back where they slipped down into his scuffed shoes.

"I'm sure you've had a nice vacation," I began. "Let's tell what we liked best about Christmas." Realizing that all children don't fare equally with old St. Nick, I made a point of saying, "What you liked best about Christmas doesn't have to be your presents, but if it is, only name one thing."

I began at the end of the row farthest from Frankie. The first boy liked his new football. The second had new skis. The next boy had gone to Disneyland. Trying to compete with Disneyland, the fourth boy began a quick recital, "A race car, a drum, microscope . . . . " I stopped him short. "Remember, only one thing."

Then, Frankie started to cry quietly. I didn't need to ask the cause of his tears. I berated myself for foolishly choosing this activity, as I desperately sought for a way to rescue him.

I remembered that he had whispered to me that a new baby sister was born a few days before Christmas. "That's it!" I thought. I said, "Frankie had the best Christmas of all! He had a new baby sister. What could be more special?" Frankie was not comforted. He shouted, "I hate Santa Claus! He never came to my house this year."

That evening I told some friends about Frankie. It seemed that the Grinch had stolen Christmas for good as we sat in post-holiday gloom. Then someone suggested that maybe we could do something. Christmas for the Wilsons would be a little late, that's all. All the giddiness of the holiday season returned as we set off on a belated Christmas shopping spree. We loaded the presents in two large boxes, and on one of the boxes was taped this note:

Dear Wilson Children:

I am sorry your Christmas is late this year. When we started off on Christmas Eve, Rudolph had a cold. Just over Alaska he sneezed something awful, and almost tipped my sleigh over. We didn't realize it at the time, but I guess some of your presents spilled out. Some Eskimos found them and brought them to the North Pole by dog sled. Tonight I'm making a special trip to Utah to bring them to you.

Love, S. Claus.

Then we were off in an old 1952 Chevrolet to play Santa. We stopped in front of the house next to the Wilsons'. Turning our collars up like spies, we cast exaggerated glances around us and stealthily sneaked our way through the frigid January dusk. Silently we set the box down on the Wilson doorstep and rang the doorbell. Then it was dash away, dash away, dash away all.

But someone must have spied the getaway car "ere we drove out of sight," for the next morning Frankie burst into my classroom. "Teacher, SANTA CLAUS! He came last night in a brown Chevy!" ❄

Man with the camera
By Kathleen Chipman

I KNEW MONTHS BEFORE that this Christmas would be different from all the others. As I had grown up, the middle child in a family of ten children, my Christmases had all been centered around my family.

It was a time to be together, a time of drawing names and buying presents and wrapping them on the sly, a time of making sugar cookies and decorating them in an attempt to create a work of art as well as a tasty morsel, a time to have the traditional Christmas Eve Family Home Evening when we read out of the book of Luke.

Christmas always was a time that brought our large family together. As we grew up and apart, this time of year always joined us together again. Many times it was through a phone call placed to a far-away country and with excitement we all took our turn at the receiver. Other times it was through making and sending care packages sent long months before the holiday in order to arrive on time. But no matter where any of us were at Christmas time, the spirit of the season always seemed to draw our souls together around the Christmas tree with its warm, blinking lights and sparkling tinsel.

But as I anticipated the approaching holiday, I knew things would never be the same. I was trying not to think about it, but deep inside I knew I did not look forward to Christmas this year.

In the quiet center of our busy family was my father. The part he played in our family's Christmases was always behind-the-scenes, but unmistakably the center of all we did. Even though many times someone was away from home at Christmas, my father had always been there. He was the quiet power that formed the foundation of our family circle. But this year would be different because he would not be there.

For a year and a half, I had been the one far away from home, yet in my absence my family was even closer to me. While I was gone, fate had performed one of her great mysteries and my father's life had been taken in a sudden accident. Unable to return home, I continued my work, not fully comprehending what had happened many miles away. Now I was reunited with my family and as Christmas approached, the realness of my father's death and a great longing to have him there closed in on me.

Several weeks before Christmas day, my mother expressed her concern regarding her slowness in getting her shopping done and her unpreparedness for the coming holiday. I knew she still had a lot of shopping to do, but I was also aware that she had been working on some "project" and would tell no one what it was.

She always seemed to thrive on secrets, so I didn't push her to give information regarding her confidential activities. I knew she was making something for each of us, but I had no idea what it could possibly be.

As the pile of presents under the tree grew larger, I noticed that each of us had a gift wrapped box of similar shape and size. I knew this must be the "project" Mom had been keeping secret for so long.

On Christmas morning every member of our family came to share this day together. It was the first time in many years we had all been present on this special day. But underneath my excitement, I knew it still wasn't complete without Dad. I longed to have him there, handing out the presents as he always had done. My oldest brother had assumed this responsibility and was trying hard to make it seem the same.

Obeying Mom's instructions, he waited until last to hand out her "secret" gifts. We all opened our boxes together and inside each was a notebook. As I opened the cover, I saw my life-story written through my mother's eyes, and following were pages and pages of pictures taken from slides my father had taken of me throughout the years.

There was a dedication to "the man with the camera," my father, who captured me throughout every stage of my life.

Each one of us had received a masterpiece put together by my mother. She had taken months writing her feelings about each of us, going through Dad's slides, and getting them made into prints.

We enjoyed each other's books, laughed at the pictures, and delighted in the contents, and this gift caused more enjoyment than any of the other presents we had opened, which now lay unnoticed on the floor.

I cried as I read the words my mother had written. I understood now that she had always perceived how I had felt, even when I had thought she would never understand certain things I had gone through.

I felt her love for each of her children and especially for her husband, my father, "the man with the camera," whose influence and presence was never felt more strongly than on this, my most memorable Christmas day.

Honesty's reward

By Thomas J. Griffiths

HE YEAR WAS 1916 and I was eight years old. While it happened long ago, it is still the Christmas I remember best.

Our family lived in a little village in Wales that went by the quaint name of Old Furnace. Our family consisted of Mam and Dad and eight children. The youngest was Ivor John, who was born two months early and was still a sickly child.

November that year was colder than usual. There was rain and snow with a cruel north wind that cut like a knife. One day while walking home from his work at the colliery, Dad found a woman's purse just outside the big iron gate of the Tredegar estate. He opened it and found that it belonged to Lady Tredegar. Beside her identification there was a roll of paper money that was more than Dad had ever seen at one time.

He took the money in his hand and thought of all the things it would buy, especially with Christmas approaching.

But he had been trained to be honest, so he returned the money to the purse and swung open the big iron gate. Lady Tredegar received him quite casually and after counting the money, and finding it all there, inquired of his name and where he lived.

"You are an honest man and it shall not be forgotten," she said, and then motioned to the butler to show him out.

As Dad continued homeward, he fumed that Lady Tredegar had not given him a small reward. He was still angry when he entered our cottage and told mother of the incident.

In her Welsh dialect, she spoke to my father: "Indeed now, it's an honest man you are, and God will not forget."

As November came to a close, the bitter cold took its toll and Dad was stricken with pneumonia. In those days there were no antibiotics or other medication to fight this disease and one could only wait for the change that would decide life or death. For a while, it looked as if he would not live to see Christmas, but one night the change came.

We heard him call for Mam and we children crowded around his bed. The change had come. He was in a deep sweat and the fever was leaving. He would live to see Christmas.

Those were the days, too, when there was no such thing as sick pay or unemployment insurance, so before very long the family was in dire straits. Dad was still weak and it would be some time before he could return to work.

A few days before Christmas, Mam called the family together in the living room and explained that because of Dad's illness, there was no money for Christmas gifts, except for one. "Dad is still with us," she added.

Christmas Eve came and as we sat by the fireside we could hear the voices of the carolers in the distance, and over the cold frosty air came the chimes of the bells of Trevethin Church.

Dad was sitting in his big leather chair, his feet by the fire with Mam's shawl over his lap. He looked around at his family and with a voice touched by emotion, he said: "We have no gifts to give this year, but God has given us voices so let us sing of Bethlehem and the birth of Jesus."

So, as a family, we blended our voices and sang the songs of Christmas. As we were singing, there was the sound of horses' hooves on the road outside. They stopped in front of our house. Then came a knock at the door. Mam answered and there, with a huge basket in his arms, was Lady Tredegar's butler. He put the basket on the kitchen table and returned to the waiting carriage. He came back with a second basket as full as the first.

As he turned to leave he said to Mam, "Lady Tredegar wishes an honest man a Merry Christmas."

Eagerly, the baskets were opened and an array of gifts was uncovered. There was a warm jacket for Dad and gloves in the pocket, a blue dress for Mam and gifts for the children. In the second basket was a huge goose surrounded by fruits from many lands.

This was the best Christmas I remember best and one that will never be forgotten.

Sharing Christmas

By Terri Lynn Johnson

"CAROL, YOUR HEART'S BIGGER than your home," a friend told my mom upon learning we were sponsoring a Laotian refugee family of six just three days before Christmas 1979.

With only a one-day notice, we worried she would be right. My 17-year-old brother hastily vacated his basement bedroom for a living room sofa so two of the Laotians could use his room. The others slept in the adjacent family room on mattresses spread on the floor. None spoke English except the father, who told us that for the past 15 months they had lived in a Thailand refugee camp room so small only five could lie down at once; consequently, he had sat up nights. Our home instantly appeared larger.

The day after they arrived, we invited them to church with us. As my dad conducted the meeting and introduced the family, I glanced at the congregation and saw smiles and sympathy on their faces. Afterwards, our High Priest group leader, wanting to involve others, passed out copies of the refugees' names, ages, and sizes. Soon people began pouring into our home in a steady stream of caring, bearing gifts and promises of dental work and furniture. I remembered Christ's words: "Inasmuch as ye have done it unto one of the least of these my brethren, ye have done it unto me."

The next morning, Christmas Eve, a young family took four of the Laotians shopping and bought them shoes, toys and a coat for the mother. When they returned, my mom, thrilled at their generosity, exclaimed, "Have a Merry Christmas!" The wife's voice shook, "We already have." As Mom wiped a tear from her eye, I understood: "It is more blessed to give than to receive."

A Cub Scout arrived with a big well-kept Tonka truck and handed it to an excited Laotian boy. Later the scout's mother confided: "It was his favorite toy; he wanted to give his very best."

One lady brought a box of used items and a brand new blanket. I remember baby-tending for her, and finding only a near-empty jar of peanut butter and a couple of slices of bread to feed her children. I knew she had given all she could, and I felt deeply touched as the meaning behind Christ's example of the widow's mite flooded into my mind.

An immigrant family from Germany offered them new beds and linen. The mother explained, "When we first came to America, people were very kind to us; this is our way of repaying that debt." Christ's words again echoed in my heart: "As I have loved you, love one another."

That night we told the family of our Christmas traditions. The father, fascinated, in turn told us how he had escaped from a communist work camp in Laos. Two fellow escapees had died in the attempt. Freedom was priceless!

Early Christmas morning we hurriedly opened our presents, then raced downstairs to watch the refugees. The 8-year-old waltzed around the room, displaying her new dresses, as her 9-year-old brother emptied his Christmas stocking onto the floor, sending a cascade of treasures to the four corners of the room.

Little 2-year-old Jimmy (named for President Carter) clutched onto a stuffed cow until he heard music. Tracing the sounds to a small box, he pressed the keys and heard more music. He smiled, the first emotion I had seen on his face other than fear. I wanted to play with him, but when I reached out, he hid behind his mother.

The 15-year-old boy, my age, eagerly ripped open a thousand-piece puzzle unaware of the importance of the picture guide, which was destroyed. Nevertheless, we managed to put the puzzle together.

For the next two weeks, my three brothers and sisters and I played with the children while my mom took the father out looking for employment and an apartment. Mealtimes seemed hectic, integrating two menus and 13 people, but we learned to like "sticky" rice, and they began drinking milk — sweetened. As their fear, confusion and anxiety diminished, we became lasting friends.

Throughout that Christmas vacation I watched a miracle unfold. I saw strangers accepted into a free land, leaving behind all their family, friends, and possessions; and I saw followers of Christ shower them with love. I grew from witnessing and then experiencing that love myself, and I know now that giving of oneself is the best way to celebrate Christ's birth. My desire is to exemplify the teaching: "When ye are in the service of your fellow beings ye are only in the service of your God" — not just a Christmas, but all my life.

A Christmas friend

By Connie Wilcox

HRISTMAS WAS ALWAYS EXCITING in my hometown while I was growing up, but one Christmas has been remembered more than the others because that is the time that I gained a very dear friend.

I recall the year of my 4th grade, a month before Christmas and Emmy Lou Soper. We became friendly, I think, mostly because she was so sad and shy and didn't have any friends. We talked a little, but usually we just smiled at each other. I was always happy to see those faded blue and white striped overalls coming through the school door each day. Sometimes she brought something to chew on for lunch, but most of the time she didn't. At first she would not share my food, but it was not long before she overcame her shyness — as far as food was concerned — and ate as if she were starved.

Each evening after school that December, I could do nothing but talk about Emmy Lou. For some reason I couldn't get her out of my mind. After a while mom related a sad story about the family. The father had been a drunkard, a child abuser and a molester. The authorities had somehow found this out and had kicked him out of town. In the 1940s, I guess they didn't know what else to do. There were two older sisters who were sent to live with relatives in another town, which left Emmy Lou and her mother alone. Emmy Lou was young at the time, and nothing more had been said about the family.

Mom had seen Mrs. Soper from time to time in town shopping for groceries. They always said hello to each other, but she had not seen Mrs. Soper recently.

Just before Christmas, Emmy Lou started missing school quite frequently, and when she did come she was extremely quiet and pale and would hardly accept any lunch. It was so disturbing that I could hardly talk about anything else, which was unusual for me that close to Christmas.

Christmas was a special time in our family. We baked, shopped, decorated and cut Christmas trees in the mountains. I looked forward to our annual trip up Joe's Gap with dad to cut trees. He gave trees to the widows, the poor families and to the church. The rest of the trees he would sell — which always supplied the money for our Christmas. Somehow this particular Christmas, my spirit just wasn't the same.

Emmy Lou didn't come to school at all the week before the Christmas holiday. I asked the teacher about her, but she didn't know anything and the kids didn't seem to care. Mom and Dad could see how distressed I was becoming, and finally father said, "Well, dear, if it will help, let's just get in the truck and drive out there. There is still a Christmas tree left so let's just take it out to them." Mom packed up a basket of food and said she had prepared way too much for our family, suggesting that maybe Emmy Lou and her mother could use it.

The ride was very long or at least is seemed that way. The truck moved slowly because the snow was unplowed and very deep, but we finally arrived. I have never felt such anxiety in my life as I looked around the desolate place. It was nothing but a broken down old house with a shack in back that had probably been a chicken coop. There was no life, and the undisturbed snow was deep right up to the door. I think the most haunting memory of all was the fact that no smoke was coming out of the chimney.

Shakily, I jumped out of the truck, and I caught a worried glimpse in my father's eyes. I knocked on the door, but no answer. I knocked harder and louder and was becoming frantic as I peeked in the window. It was getting dark, and I could barely see Emmy Lou laying on the bed. But she did not respond when I yelled to her. I tried the door; it was unlocked so I went in.

"Emmy Lou, Emmy Lou, where have you been? Why haven't you been to school?" I looked down on the bed and for a split second I thought I was looking at a corpse. It was Mrs. Soper. She turned her head slowly, opened her eyes, lifted her hand and said "Help me." She then dropped her hand and lay very still. Emmy Lou was crying and said "Mama's going to die, and I haven't been able to leave her." The house was cold and empty and sad. We had so much, but they had nothing.

Father started building a fire — he always knew the right thing to do — and brought in the food. Mom had sent a quart of her famous Christmas turkey bone soup and I proceeded to warm it. Dad turned and as he went for the door he said, "I'm going for the doctor."

It was about an hour before he returned with Doc Rich (he brought me into the world, repaired a broken arm, and removed my tonsils). I was sitting by Emmy Lou, and she was clutching my hand but had stopped crying. Doc Rich confirmed that Mrs. Soper was very ill and should probably go to the hospital so he could keep an eye on her, but assured us that she wouldn't die. However, if we hadn't arrived there when we did there would not have been a chance for her.

Dr. Rich and Dad bundled her up and carried her to the truck while we climbed in, too. Dad dropped us off at our home and said that he and Doc would take care of everything.

That Christmas was a Christmas I will never forget because Emmy Lou stayed with us for two weeks — all through the Christmas holiday. I shared all my clothes and raked up an extra pair of ice skates and a sleigh. We played and laughed and had fun and got to be best friends. We also visited her mom everyday, too. A miracle actually took place in Mrs. Soper because we could see a sad, desolate face change into one with a pleasant, contented expression.

The most amazing miracle of all is that Santa Claus knew Emmy Lou was at our house and brought both of us exactly the same things. I was puzzled and happy about that for years.

A greater power
By Kenneth J. Brown

I WATCHED HIM TURN from the street and climb the path leading to our shelter. He was groping, hesitating. As he came near he folded his umbrella and stood quietly a long moment. His thin coat soon dampened from the cold rain that was falling from the same sky that had brought death to nearly half his townspeople three short months before. I concluded that it must take some special courage to confront one's conquerors without invitation. It was little wonder that he hesitated.

His polite bow to me was no bow of submission. Rather his squared shoulders and lifted head let me feel as if I were looking up at him even more though I towered over him a foot or more. I recall being disturbed that I hadn't yet become used to the near sightless eyes of those who had looked heavenward that morning when the bomb dropped. If one looked deeply enough he could almost see the reflection of a searing, blinding flash in those eyes.

Dignity commands respect in all quarters and I respectfully asked if I could be of service. His clear English told me that his educational pursuits had taken him beyond the home islands. He introduced himself as Professor Iida. The title fit him well.

"I am Christian," he said. "I am told this is the head minister's office. Are you a Christian? It is good to talk with a follower of Christ; there are so few Christian Japanese."

I took him to the inner office of the division chaplain and waited while the two men conversed. Professor Iida stated his request briefly. He was a teacher of music in a Christian girls' college until it was closed by imperial command. Afterward he had been imprisoned because of his professed Christianity. After being released he had returned to Nagasaki and continued his music instruction in his home even though it was forbidden. He had been able to continue a small chorus and would be pleased if it could be arranged that they sing a concert for the American Marines.

"We know something of your American Christmases," he said. "We should like to do something to make your Christmas in Japan more enjoyable."

I felt sure the chaplain would give a negative reply. Our unit was one of hardened fighters, four years away from home, who had fought the enemy from Saipan to Iwo Jima. Their hatred had hardly had time to cool. A troupe of girls appearing before them on stage, perhaps daughters or sisters of the ones who had killed their buddies, might provoke an incident humiliating to the occupation authorities. Yet there was something about the man that bespoke sincere desire to do a good deed so that his request could hardly be denied.

Permission was granted. The concert would be Christmas Eve.

The rains had stopped and a calm settled over the atomic bowl reminiscent of the calm that night long ago. The concert was well attended; there was nothing else to do. The theater, now turned amphitheater, had been cleared of its fallen roof and men were sitting on the jagged walls. The usual momentary hush fell over the audience as the performers filed on stage. As the music began the hush swelled to complete silence that strangely lasted the hour.

The first thing we noticed was that they were singing in English and we became aware that they didn't understand the words but had memorized them for our benefit. Professor Iida had taught his students well; they sang beautifully. We sat enthralled as if a choir from heaven were singing for us. Of course, it was wonderful to hear those familiar carols again, yet it wasn't so much what they sang; it was as if Christ were being born anew that night.

The closing number was a solo, an aria from "The Messiah." The girl sang with all the conviction of one who knew that Jesus was indeed the Savior of mankind and it brought tears. After that there was a full minute of silence followed by sustained applause as the small group took bow after bow.

Later that night I helped Professor Iida take down the trimmings. I could not resist asking some questions that propriety forbade but curiosity demanded. I just had to know.

"How did your group manage to survive the bomb?" I asked.

"This is only half my group," he said softly, but seemed unoffended at my recalling his grief so that I felt I could ask more.

"And what of the families of these?"

"They nearly all lost one or more members. Some are orphans."

"What about the soloist? She must have the soul of an angel the way she sang."

"Her mother, two of her brothers were taken. Yes, she did sing well; I am so proud of her. She is my daughter, you know."

The next day was Christmas, the one I remember best. For that day I knew that Christianity had not failed in spite of people's unwillingness to live His teachings. I had seen hatred give way to service, pain to rejoicing, sorrow to forgiveness. This was possible because a babe had been born in a manger who later taught love of God and fellowmen. We had caused them the greatest grief and yet we were their Christian brothers and as such they were willing to forget their grief and unite with us in singing "Peace on earth, good will to all men."

The words of Miss Iida's song testimony would not be stilled, "Surely he hath borne our griefs, and carried our sorrows." They seemed to echo and re-echo over the half-dead city that day.

That day also I knew that there was a greater power on earth than the atomic bomb.

A hair-raising tale
By Peggy M. Cook

NGELA WAS VERY BEAUTIFUL. She had long golden curls, big blue eyes that opened and closed and long silky lashes. I named her Angela because to me she looked just like an angel. In fact, to a four-year-old girl she was the most beautiful doll in the whole world, but this was long ago. The year 1925, the place, Norwich, England; it was almost Christmas.

As I have mentioned, Angela was very beautiful, but that was before I decided to cut her hair. Mother had recently taken me to the hairdresser to get my hair cut "so it would look extra special for Christmas." Why shouldn't Angela's hair look extra special, too?

I thought maybe I should first get mother's opinion. Just then there came a knock at the door. It was mother's best friend. Oh dear, I couldn't get mother's attention now. Without hesitation I decided to cut Angela's hair.

I smiled to myself picturing how surprised mother would be when she saw Angela's lovely new hair-do. Quickly I went to the parlor. I lost no time with scissors and comb and a doll's beautiful hair. One by one, the lovely locks fell. I don't know how it happened, but suddenly I realized I had snipped off more hair than I had intended. I didn't know where to stop. By this time Angela did not look exactly as I had expected. In fact, she didn't look like Angela at all. Neither did she resemble an angel.

Just as I was thinking I had made a mistake, mother walked in. She was smiling. The smile vanished when she saw my doll. "What have you done to Angela?" she cried. "Whatever will auntie say?"

Years later I learned at what personal sacrifice this gift had been purchased for me by my wonderful aunt. In 1925 I understood none of this. When auntie did find out she wasn't angry. She even seemed amused. I was comforted by the knowledge that Angela's hair would grow again. Of course it would! Mine always did. I had a hard time convincing mother. Oh well, she would see. In the meanwhile I would hide Angela. Just until her hair grew. After wrapping her in a warm blanket, I tucked her in bed, and left her in the parlor.

About this time every year my dad had an annoying habit of locking the parlor door. No matter how I pleaded, it was all in vain. I was not allowed inside. This tradition was observed for many years. Not once in the years to follow did I yearn to get inside that room as I did then.

How could I find out how Angela's hair was growing with the parlor off limits until Christmas morning? This was a dire emergency. How could my own dad attach such little importance to something he knew meant so much to his little girl? I was very disappointed in his lack of feeling.

Behind that locked door my dad worked long hours each evening decorating around the fireplace and other areas of the room. He also trimmed the Christmas tree, as only he knew how. Beautiful glass ornaments preserved from many years before were brought out of their carefully padded boxes and hung on the tree. Icicles that shimmered and shone were also part of the decorations. Then there were tiny colored glass lanterns. Each lantern held in its center a miniature candle. The candles were lit only under strict supervision because of the fire hazard.

The days dragged that week before Christmas, but finally the long-awaited day dawned.

On Christmas Eve in England children would hang their stocking on the bedpost for Father Christmas to fill. It was barely light when I awakened. Father Christmas had been there already. I could tell by the way my stocking bulged. Excitedly, I grabbed it, and made for downstairs.

The parlor door was open. I could see Dad lighting the lanterns on the Christmas tree. Flames from the fireplace crackled and danced, transforming the room into a Christmas wonderland. Breathlessly, I tiptoed in. Then I saw her. The most wonderful sight. My Angela, more beautiful than ever, dressed in the most exquisite red velvet gown. A sparkling tiara atop her shining curls, looking ever more like an angel.

"Oh Angela," I cried, as I hugged her close to me. "You are the most beautiful doll in all the world." Just then my dad opened the window ever so slightly. He held Angela and me in one arm until the other encircled my mother. Together we listened to the church bells ringing in the glorious magic, which was Christmas, 1925.

Playing Santa Claus

By Rhea Hart Grandy

CHRISTMAS THAT YEAR promised to be something really special. I had just turned thirteen, the oldest girl and middle child in a family of eleven. My mother, recovering from the flu and not yet well enough to hitch up the horse and drive into town, had turned the Christmas shopping over to me.

"I guess if we have Christmas this year it will be up to you," she said. And then added, "Father said he would call and let us know as soon as he has some money for you."

I was elated. I knew just what I was going to buy. There would be candy and nuts, toys for the younger children (my older brothers, the "big boys" mother called them, usually bought their own presents), nothing for myself, this year I was going to sacrifice and put to the test the old preachment, "It is better to give than to receive," and most important of all, a special gift for my mother: a nice warm pair of boots; zippers they were called.

It disturbed me that for many winters she had gone bootless in the deep snow to the chicken coop and the barn to feed the chickens and pigs, gather the eggs, and milk the cow; and I intended to change that.

It was the day before Christmas. I worried the morning away waiting for father, a practicing attorney successful in attracting clients but not as successful in collecting his fees, to call from his office saying someone had paid a long overdue bill and there would be money for Christmas shopping.

The afternoon came and was rapidly wearing on. I had about given up in despair when he finally called to say someone had given him ten dollars.

I immediately donned my coat and rubbers, and in the growing dusk of that slightly snowy Christmas Eve set out on the two-mile trek to town.

Selecting the prized boots was no problem — small matter that they cost five dollars, half of what father had given me — but finding something for the children was not so easy. The merchants' shelves were distressingly bare — not that I could have bought very much with what money was left. I finally chose one large but quite unique wind-up toy that I thought all of the children could enjoy. A bag of nuts and some hard-tack candy completed my purchases. At the last moment a small bottle of perfume overruled my resolve to buy nothing for myself, and my remaining ten cents went for that.

The children were not yet to bed when I arrived home, and since the cumbersome packages, by now dog-eared and half open, had revealed most of their secrets anyway, we decided to have a Christmas Eve Christmas.

The children were quite intrigued by the marvelous toy, and they laughed and giggled joyfully over its amusing antics. But it was not so with mother. We all gathered around when the big moment came when she was to open her package. I was expecting a big show of pleasure and delight when she saw the much-needed gift. But she wasn't pleased at all. In fact she was greatly displeased, and I was completely shaken by her reaction.

"Zipper Boots!" she cried, throwing them angrily aside. "What a foolish thing to do. I won't have them. They must go back to the store the day after Christmas."

If ever a child was hurt, it was I. I was crushed. Heartsick, let down, dejected. I almost gave way to tears. Had I not been led to believe, by an older brother, that tears were for sissies, they most certainly would have spilled over.

Later, crestfallen and blue, I placed the magical toy under the sad but comical looking Christmas tree — a crayon colored cardboard star and a few homemade red and green paper chains, its only ornamentation. Comical because, unable to interest any of my brothers in making a stand for it, I had tackled the job myself. Although I managed to get it upright, it leaned crazily to one side, threatening to crash at the slightest touch, reminding one when it teetered and rocked of a big, clumsy, down-at-the-heels old boozer, three sheets to the wind.

Christmas morning the children rediscovered the wonderful toy, played with it for a while, then eventually lost interest and went on to other pursuits. The small bottle of perfume was but little consolation for the disappointment I was harboring. All morning I moped about the house absorbed in gloom, nursing my wounded pride.

Then a marvelous thing happened. Santa Claus came after all. My oldest brother and his wife, newlywed of just about one month, came bearing gifts. There was a gaily wrapped present for everyone, including me. I could hardly believe my eyes. Instantly all was smiles and sunshine. My spirits soared again; my world righted itself.

I watched with interest as each child opened his gift and noting the sudden glow on each face. Eagerly I opened my present and discovered to my delight the most beautiful strand of beads I had ever seen — opaque, delicate orange in color and cleverly designed to charm a young girl's heart. I had never been more thrilled!

I suppose our Mr. and Mrs. Santa Claus never fully realized the joy they brought into our house that day with their basket of gifts or the impact their kindness had on me. I have long since forgotten what the other children received, but my gift I treasured for years. When the beads eventually became a keepsake only, I still loved and cherished them — and remembered.

As for the "better to give than to receive" philosophy, I guess at age thirteen I was not yet ready for that timeless bit of wisdom, but my mother, the most unselfish of women, was and would have willingly gone bootless in the snow for many more years rather than have the children miss Christmas.

Now, years later, and a mother myself, I understand.

Santa Claus boycotted

By Dorothy See

AMONG THE TREASURES STORED in my memory bank are my recollections of Norwich before the fire. A small village in Southeastern Ohio, Norwich was strung along the old National Road, halfway between Cambridge and Zanesville.

This was an ideal arrangement, as my paternal grandparents and my mother's aunts, uncles and cousins were 12 miles to the east in Cambridge, while my father's aunts, uncles and cousins dwelt 12 miles to the west. Either way we went, I was surrounded with affection.

Norwich, itself, was a picturesque hamlet of 19th century farmhouses and quiet church yards. Sometimes when my mother, teen-age Aunt Frances and I went berry picking or nut gathering we would find a roofless cabin in the sumac. The frontier, even in Ohio, was not far behind us in the 1920s.

My father had dammed up the creek in back of the cow pasture, creating our own swimming pool for hot summer days.

The village school house in those days before consolidation, was a three-roomed brick affair with a pump on the lawn and a tin cup in each desk. Four grades were assigned to each room.

The highlight of the year was always Christmas, when every resident, regardless of religious persuasion, would go to the Methodist Church in the center of town. There a huge, candle-lit tree would contain a small gift for every person.

The Christmas I was six promised to be the best one ever. Santa Claus in his sleigh, pulled by six reindeer, was to be in Zanesville — where we could actually see him instead of trying to stay awake all night to catch a glimpse as he dropped down our narrow chimney. We all looked forward to it!

In late November, two weeks before the great event, a Norwich farmer, more familiar with his team than his Model T Ford, lit a match to see if he had gas in his tank. He did. The converted barn with a full hay loft overhead burst into flames that consumed outbuildings as well as the barn and contents, then roared on to devour the ancient inn where the stagecoaches, then buses, had stopped for a hundred years.

Unsatisfied, and fanned by high winds, the fire consumed the town hall and moved on to a general store and overhead apartments.

In Cambridge, my grandparents saw the glow in the western sky, hours after sunset and called the Norwich telephone operator who babbled from her dining room switchboard, "It is burning! It's all burning!"

My grandfather summoned the Cambridge Fire Department which dispatched two pumpers.

The operator had already called the Zanesville Fire Department, which told her a city ordinance prevented them from sending fire equipment beyond the town limits.

All through the bitterly cold night the men battled the flames while the women formed bucket brigades to the icy wells and waited for help that would never come. The largest Cambridge pumper broke down as it crossed the bridge leaving town. The smaller, older pumper limped on through the night with help that would be too little and too late.

My brother and I slept through it all behind blankets our mother had pinned over our beds. We awoke to a world of stark, bare chimneys, charred timbers and ashes. Our house had been spared because a stone barn had stood between us and the path of the flames.

With the sunrise came bitterness against Zanesville that had refused to help. The whole town of Norwich agreed to boycott the stores in that city.

Our first grade class received this information with horror. A boycott of Zanesville at this time was a boycott of Santa Claus, Comet, Dancer, Prancer, Blitzen, Donner and Vixen and all the rest.

For the next few days the 14 members of the first grade class shuffled through the ash-laden snow — with the acrid odor of charred wood in our noses and solid lead in our hearts.

No amount of pleading or cajoling created any signs of relenting on the part of our parents, who apparently couldn't understand that Santa Claus — with reindeer — was the realization of our dreams.

We ate breakfast glumly the day he was to arrive in the nearby town, and stared moodily from our windows at the bare chimneys.

In our disappointment, we didn't question our parents later when they shoved us into our unyielding winter attire and into the Gardner touring car with isinglass side curtains. We huddled under lap robes as the car sped at 30 mph — westward . . . to Zanesville!

There we saw him — and his sleigh — and the reindeer! And he was just like we had known he would be — a right jolly old elf, waving and smiling at us as we stood in the snowy slush of Zanesville's Main Street. It was wonderful!

But he wasn't all we saw that day in the crowded streets. All through the crowds we saw familiar faces — familiar Norwich faces. All the people of Norwich who were supposed to be boycotting the town were there on the street. I know the entire first grade class members, with their parents, brothers and sisters were there.

We all pretended we hadn't seen each other. And for 50 years afterward no one ever mentioned that they went that day to see Santa Claus — until now. ❄

Bear was there, too!
By Mrs. Farren Keyte

HERE IS A SAYING that Christmas is for children. I had heard that statement when I was younger and had laughed, for everyone knew, if they were aware at all, that Christmas was for fun. It was for parties and tobogganing. It was wondering who would ask you out for the holidays. It was the exquisite consideration of the large box with the velvet bow . . . the one with your name on it!

One wonderful year it was an engagement ring slipped lovingly on a trembling finger, the warmth of a kiss that held heaven and earth seen through misty eyes. However, the memory on that Christmas was lost in the excitement of a wedding that followed soon after.

I distinctly remember the eight Christmases after that as they all lump dimly together. Oh, the first Christmas as a wife was fun and new. I remember that alright. But at that time, we were close to our families and were welcomed to two circles instead of our former one. The following years, however, found us farther away and just we two. Funny how quiet a Christmas morning is with only two. Yes, those were eight childless, vacant years.

We both worked. We bought a new car, a new boat, new furniture. Yet somehow the satisfaction of our well-being couldn't keep that lump from my throat as I held a neighbor's child and felt a small soft arm surround my neck. What is there in this world really without children?

Well, for us there were many trips to doctors. Each new referral brought hope that our childless state was only temporary. At last it was the terrible finality of facing the truth. We would bear no children. It was a brick wall so high, so thick and so solid, there was seemingly no way to pass by it. It was something you tried to accept and live with, but somehow the tears that slipped into your pillow each night would not believe.

I would say our decision to adopt a child was an inevitable one for us and certainly a necessary one to replace despair with hope. I can't say I remember that first Christmas after becoming an "instant mother" as our son was too small to know what it was all about. I remember better the month of May two years later when we brought home a baby sister to round out our family.

A merry hubbub of years then followed changing us from young marrieds, to doting parents, to harried housewife and an overtime Dad. Along the way our compact, routine world changed accordingly.

Then one day of days we had a first grader! We were deluged with painting, ABC's, papers with lopsided print, and wonder of wonders, our boy could read! Our world would never be the same again.

Another Christmas was on its way. Lists were drawn up for Santa and excitement was in the air. One evening at supper our school boy proudly announced a "project" at school. But it was secret, very secret. He couldn't tell, not even young sister because she couldn't be trusted. He must have a box to take to school, just a small box, one in which he could wrap his very special gift to us.

We smiled. This was so new . . . a secret he was bursting with, yet holding on to with giant determination. We smiled again. This was more like the Christmas of old, with secret packages being slipped under the tree. This time from a totally unexpected source . . . our child!

I bought a creche that year. Strange I'd never thought about one before, but this year the two youngsters in our family would be made aware of just what Christmas really meant. I wanted something durable, not just cardboard figures, one that would last for other years. Our few tree ornaments and lights really didn't constitute a family tradition and we were truly a family now. The creche I settled on was a wooden stable with the usual figures of Mary, the Babe, and Joseph. There was one wiseman, one shepherd, two lambs and a donkey. Not quite as many figures as I desired but it had a lovely built-in music box that played a tinkling version of Silent Night. I knew instinctively the children would enjoy that part.

That evening I got it out and let the children place it on a table. The music box was an instant success and we heard many renditions of its tune as each child took a turn at winding again and again. I supervised the placement of the figures and when I was satisfied with their appearance I went on to other things. Later when I felt the saturation point of "Silent Night" had been reached I returned to suggest the children desist. I found them still kneeling by the small table arranging and rearranging the scene. The small figures seemed to present endless possibilities to them.

"The animals loved Baby Jesus, didn't they Momma? That's why there are animals here, isn't it?" My son's eyes were bright.

"That's really a nice observation, dear. I hadn't thought about it much before, but I'm sure they did. It's certainly true the donkey did his part in carrying Mary, and the shepherds must have brought the lambs . . . yes, I think we could safely say the animals were happy to see the Baby Jesus, too."

"And there were other animals, too, weren't there?"

I thought a moment about that question. You never really know what will pop up in a conversation with children or just what answer their small minds are seeking. Looking back I'm glad I answered just as I did.

"Yes, there were other animals. The camels came with the wisemen and there were probably some cows in the stable."

A smile a mile wide glowed upon his face. "I thought so!" Then in a moment he was gone to play at a new interest.

Christmas morning came just as the children could bear the suspense no more and happily before the big secret of the mysterious package had escaped. As soon as the scramble and squeals of discovery subsided our sturdy six-year-old tenderly retrieved the small box he had placed under the tree. He brought it and placed it in my lap.

"Open mine first, will you Momma! I know you will like it!"

I looked down at a smudgy square box, literally scotch-taped to the teeth, but unmistakenly Christmasy with a large bow on top. The tag barely had room for the large scrawl, "To Mom, Dad, Gina . . . from Leslie," it read. Everything stopped while the very special box was opened. I had no previous experience with first grade projects and wondered what he could possibly have made to produce the shining eyes and smile of anticipation before me now.

The paper fell away, the lid was removed in a hushed silence. I looked rather blankly at a small, lumpy, black object within. I shot a glance at my husband for help, meanwhile lifting it up with," Oh!, Look, isn't it lovely! Did you really make this all by yourself?"

My husband joined in, "Why look at that! Why don't you tell us all about it?"

"It's nice, isn't it! It's a bear!" He took it into his small hand barely evolved from its chubby baby fat and turned it this way and that with pride. "See, these are his ears and the two blue dots are his eyes. I molded it and painted it myself. I think mine was the best one, some of the others, you couldn't even tell what they were!"

Now our enjoyment was genuine with the relief of knowing what we were admiring. Yes, you could make out a bear with sturdy legs (or a rhinoceros, as my husband laughed later.)

"And I know just where to put it!" He walked to the small Christmas scene on the table and moving the shepherd and the lamb back he placed his lumpy black bear close by the Baby Jesus. "A bear would have wanted to see the Baby Jesus, too, wouldn't he?" We hugged and nodded our response, unable to speak, as his blue eyes shone with the simple plausibility of the very young.

That was the first addition to our sparse creche, since then we have added an angel, two small green trees, and one more wiseman. We have in mind to add the other wiseman and camel this year.

By now our shcool boy is a big 4th grader, but he still places the lumpy black bear close to the Baby Jesus. He looks up shyly, remembering, "You liked it didn't you?"

"We really did. You sure surprised us that Christmas!" And we all smile at each other for it's that lovely time of year again and we are a family and we have a real family tradition.

Yes, it's really true. Christmas is for and because of children. ✻

Mike in the nick of time
By Mrs. Erna Park

HEN I WAS A LITTLE GIRL, we lived out on a farm in what is now called South Salt Lake. We had been begging Dad for a dog, just any kind of a dog. One day he walked in the house, all smiles. We rushed to greet him and felt something wiggly under his overcoat. With squeals, we begged to see. After teasing us for a while, he pulled out from underneath his overcoat the cutest little ball of fur you could imagine.

At the sight of him, we went wild and so did the puppy. It was love at first sight and we all had a wonderful time. He was about the sweetest, wildest terrier we had ever seen. He had a way of getting deep down in your heart and he gave us, too, all the love in the world. "Mike," as we called him, became a part of our family right from the start.

He romped and played with us kids and wherever we went so did he. He wrestled with us, raced with us and whatever we played he always had to get in the act. When spring came and baseball was in the air, he played that too. He became quite a good shortstop, too, but sometimes he got a little wild and ran away with the ball. Then it was our turn to chase him and this gave him a lot of pleasure. We couldn't get mad at him, we had too much fun. The only time we'd leave him home is when we'd take a ride in the old Ford. He pouted like a child when we left him behind. But we could always be sure he'd be waiting for us with his waggly tail when we returned.

One day we got into the car and went into Salt Lake City to do some shopping for Thanksgiving. The snow was deep and it had turned bitter cold. We looked back to see Mike sitting on the step watching us leave and I remember feeling a twinge of regret at having to leave him behind. When we finished our shopping, Dad decided to take us to the show. That was quite a treat and we were all happy.

On the way home we all sang songs and the car was filled with laughter and song. When we arrived home, all piled out of the car, but no white streak greeted us, no happy bark called to us. Mike was gone. We were an unhappy bunch, as we called and searched, and Dad took the car and hunted for hours, but none of us saw any sign of him. The happiness had gone out of our day. We felt sure if he were alive, he'd return to us. But, as the days turned into weeks only a faint glimmer of hope remained that we'd ever see our Mike again.

Christmas Eve came and trimming the tree was a family affair. We finished putting on our ornaments and stringed popcorn; the final touch was turning on the lights. It was a lovely tree and, with its lighting, Mom turned to the piano and started to play the favorite carols and we all joined our voices in song.

Suddenly, in the midst of a song, Mom stopped playing for a moment. We all just looked at each other, for we'd all heard a faint whining sound. Then as one we rushed to the door. There with loving eyes was our beloved Mike. The remains of a rope was around his neck and he was the dirtiest, most bedraggled looking mutt you ever saw, but to us he was the most beautiful sight in the world — he'd come back to us. His little paws were worn and bleeding, but he seemed to say, "I made it home to you." With the return of Mike it turned out to be a most wonderful Christmas and the one I remember best. Christmas morning Mike had a companion, for there was another ball of white fur under the Christmas tree. But to us all, there would only be one Mike and I'm sure he knew it too.

Christmas spirit takes time

By Alan DeMann

A ROUTINE EXPERIENCE. THAT'S WHAT IT appeared to be.

It concluded a year later as anything but routine! And it taught me some things I'll remember the rest of my life.

I was sixteen and a junior at Murray High School. A few weeks before Christmas 1975, the student body officers at the school received a letter from the Jordan Valley School asking some of our students to participate with theirs in a snow-sculpturing contest. I was among the Murray students asked to take part.

The day arrived and so did we.

As we entered Jordan Valley School, we were still not totally certain about the purpose of our visit. We were simply to work with some of the students at the school.

It was only shortly after we arrived that we were told they were mentally and physically handicapped.

But, that problem was quickly solved. We immediately put two of our group in charge of "tending" the 15 handicapped youths assigned to us. The rest of us began to work on our sculpture.

We were intent on attaining our goal: To win the contest and the trophy that went with it. To do so, we decided to take turns "tending" our new friends, while the rest of us concentrated on winning the prize. Finally, the time for judging arrived. To our surprise, we lost. Dejection and fatigue traveled home with us.

As we discussed our disappointment enroute home, someone remarked dejectedly that it had been more fun "tending the kids."

We sat silent for a moment.

Then the realization came to all of us: Not only had we lost the contest but we had failed to achieve the ultimate goal of the entire program. We felt sick.

Fortunately for me, I was to have a second chance to learn an important lesson. It was a year later that another invitation arrived at Murray High School. Our friends at Jordan Valley School were inviting us to participate in a Christmas Tree decorating contest.

We had a chance to redeem ourselves!

Those of us who had participated the previous year met and planned for the new contest. Several days of special planning went into preparations for what we knew would be a special day with some special kids.

The long-awaited day came. We packed glue, construction paper, glitter, popcorn, cranberries, crayons and almost everything else that might be used to decorate a Christmas tree.

We were on our way.

When we arrived, we received a special surprise. The youngsters who had been with us the year before had been assigned to us again.

"Hey, kids," we thought to ourselves, "we're going to make it up to you this year. You're going to decorate YOUR tree, and we're going to help."

The decorating materials were distributed; the handicapped youngsters had a "riot." Glue, popcorn, glitter, scraps of paper and almost everything else were everywhere.

As they progressed with the decorations, I was amazed that such a cluttered, messy tree could be so beautiful.

Perhaps it was because the hearts and souls and joy and laughter of those sincere kids were so wrapped up in it.

That alone would have been enough, but later, they couldn't contain themselves. There were 15 excited telephone calls home, asking parents to come and see "our very own, beautiful Christmas tree."

When judging time came again, we knew "our" tree could never win the contest. But, it didn't matter any more!

There had been a meaningful purpose accomplished. The bringing of great joy to others by the giving of self. What we learned that day, some people might never learn in a lifetime.

The events of those Christmas days will influence my entire life:

First, I have become more grateful for a sound body and mind — things which I had previously taken for granted.

Finally, I learned the true meaning of Christmas — the joy that comes from real service — from giving of yourself to others! These are the valuable lessons learned from an experience which will long be cherished from the Christmas I remember best.

Ray of hope

By Bernice Brown

VERY CHRISTMAS AS I WATCH excited youngsters pointing out their Santa orders in department stores, my heart goes back to a frosty Christmas morning in Germany 17 years ago and a little boy who had never received a Christmas present in his life.

If it had not been for World War II, the little boy and I would never have met, for I lived on a ranch in Idaho and he on a farm in Poland!

But there was World War II and one day about a week before Christmas I found myself walking up the steps of an UNRAA camp in a village along the Rhine. As a young WAC sergeant with Army Public Relations at Seventh Army Headquarters, I had come to make arrangements for a Christmas party that our group wanted to give for the young orphans of Dachau, who were quartered there.

I love children, but I had never met one like the small, unsmiling little boy who stared up at me from the building steps. I flashed him a smile that had usually been pretty effective with children. There was no answering smile. He regarded me with neither friendliness nor hostility. In his eyes only the primitive alertness of one of the wild creatures on my father's ranch. Feeling more than slightly rebuffed, I stepped around him and went inside the building.

As I prepared to leave after completing our party plans with UNRAA lady in charge, she handed me a sheet of paper.

"Here are the names of all of our children," she said. "Why don't your girls draw names and each adopt that particular child for the party?"

"Oh, that's wonderful," I said. "Perhaps we could bring each of them a gift."

The lady smiled. "I think they might like that very much. I don't believe many of them have ever had one." She paused. "Since you have already met the children, perhaps you would like to choose your child now," she asked me.

My eyes looked at the delightful children in the room but my heart went back to the little boy on the porch steps. I described him. "He's the one I want," I said.

I'm afraid you won't find him very friendly," said my hostess, "but who can blame him. He is the one I was telling you about, the one who saw his father shot and who hid under a table when they came to drag his mother off to the ovens."

I nodded but not in comprehension. How could a ranch-fed young college coed who had never seen anything more brutal than the annual Utah State-University of Utah football game possibly understand the things that had happened to this little boy. I brushed the recital off as a nightmare, which I preferred to believe had never happened to anyone, and least of all to the solemn, endearing little boy on the steps.

The finding of a gift proved an almost impossible quest. I walked through every inch of the local PX groaning inwardly at the useless supplies of perfume, soap and Swiss scarves. What I wouldn't have given for just *one* of the toys for little boys so commonplace in the "five and ten cent stores" back home.

Finally, I settled on the only thing there was, a horribly ugly khaki-colored flashlight, price 69 cents. I wrapped it in a shoe box, tied it with string and reluctantly took it to the party.

At gift opening time, I took my package and moved over by *my* little boy. If he noticed me, he gave no sign of it. He continued to stare ahead, with far-away eyes, apparently completely unaffected by the happy squeals of nearby children.

"Here is your gift," I said, gently pushing the shoe box in front of him. He nodded, pushed it to one side and began to watch the little boy next to him unwrap his gift. He seemed to have no conception that he too might have a gift.

By coincidence, that little boy also got a flashlight. Someone showed him how to flick the switch. He dashed about the room grinning and bringing into the world a light of his own making.

As my little boy watched him he suddenly became alert. The guarded look went out of his eyes, replaced with pure, wistful admiration. Excited, I pushed the box in front of him, even putting his hands on the knots in the string. But they fell limply to his sides. He wasn't interested in the old box. He was interested in his friend's flashlight. I was beside myself with frustration. How could I tell him that he, too, had such a gift when he didn't speak the same language.

There was only one solution. Quickly, I tore off the wrapping paper, opened the box and handed him the flashlight. He took my gift with wonder, with awe, with reverence and with the first smile I ever saw him exhibit. I took myself off to the nearest corner and cried harder than I had since I was there.

Just as we were leaving, I felt a tug at my arm. There was my little boy, smiling and flicking the lighted flashlight in my face. As I looked down, he squared off, bowed and said something to me in his own tongue. What it was, I will never know. But what was in his heart needed no translation.

I never saw my little boy again. Yet every Christmas he walks with me again in memory. No matter how black the headlines or how troubled my personal life, they are always eclipsed by the memory of this little boy, bowing to me with the grace taught him by his mother, murdered for her belief in the faith of her Jewish fathers in Hitler's Germany. A little boy whose suddenly smiling eyes are telling me once again that nothing — war, death, ugliness or brutality — can ever black out that thing called "hope." It is always there waiting to be illuminated.

Sometimes even the energy stored in the batteries of a 69-cent flashlight is enough to turn it on!

Will no one help?
By Jacqueline Frushour

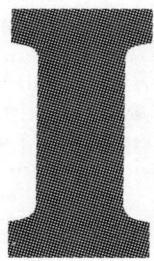

IT'S BEEN MANY YEARS NOW, but those few moments are still so vivid. I had stepped out in the backyard when a small, stray dog darted out from behind the garbage stand. When he saw me, he stopped, I looked into those soft, searching eyes; and for a long moment he returned my stare. Then without my even flinching, he turned and ran away.

I stood there wondering why, without even a word or a wave from me, he had run away. The thought came, "He ran not because he was afraid you might hurt him, but because he knew that you wouldn't help him."

That little dog was one of the reasons I found myself experiencing my first year of teaching exceptional children. When those four children first entered my classroom, I was repulsed. They were dirty; their hair was matted, and they smelled. I had to force myself to put an arm around them or to even touch them. At times when they sat next to me, I was actually nauseated; but as I grew to know them, their outward appearances began to dissolve. I began instead to see children not only deprived of food, decent clothing, and a warm place in which to live; but of love and someone who cared.

Of all my students that year, these four had the greatest effect on me. They were brothers and sister, and they carried the last name of Scar. The name was so fitting. They were slow learners academically, but they were so aware of the differences between their lives and the lives of most of the other children. So many days we would spend our scheduled time together talking.

They would tell me of what sounded like a deplorable home life. The hurt and the bitterness they expressed for a world they didn't have a place in, would sometimes overwhelm me. I would spend long, restless nights wondering how life for some could be so unfair.

Christmas was soon in the air, and I detected from them none of the excitement that the other children possessed. Not one of the four expressed even the smallest wish.

I had been saving some of my salary to fly home for the holidays, but somehow the excitement of it was escaping me. Whenever I thought of Christmas, I would see those four faces and their tattered, none-too-warm clothing.

As Christmas drew nearer, I attended a program at Church. The pine boughs, the choir, the Christmas story all helped to bring once again the beauty of Christmas. Toward the close of the program the song "Where Love Is, God Is Also" was sung. As each strain reached my ears, the images of those sad, cold, hungry children flooded before me. As the song ended, I couldn't hold back the tears. I knew then what I would do. Even if it meant no trip for Christmas, that would be one Christmas those children would find some happiness. I went home and made a list of the food, clothing and toys that I would leave in a basket on their doorstep.

As the number of days after the program began increasing, somehow my confidence in my plan was finding ways of decreasing. On one of those days the school psychologist brought winter jackets and mittens for the children. All the items were second-hand, but the happiness with which the children accepted them was something I didn't think them capable of. I realized, too, that with her gesture went half of my shopping list.

I let one of the other teachers know what I was planning, just to see what her reaction would be. She told me that if we did for all the poor students what I intended to do for the Scars, we would be poor ourselves.

Later I overheard the teachers talking about how a local organization would be sending baskets of food and toys to the needy on Christmas day. They seemed to agree that the needy children would have a fine Christmas. Hearing that, all my dreams and good intentions quickly vanished.

Needless to say, I flew home for Christmas; and I had a wonderful visit.

That first day back to school, I was scheduled for playground duty. It was cold that morning. Even through my mittens and fur-lined boots I could feel the cold. As I stomped around to warm myself, I looked up to see in the farthest corner of the play field, a small figure in a red jacket.

As the child drew nearer, I could tell that it was the youngest of the Scar children. I hurried toward him, eager to hear about his Christmas. He ran as he saw me approach, and he arrived bright-eyed and breathless. The worlds tumbled over one another as he tried to speak.

Finally he managed, "See, see, Teacher. I got a truck for Christmas!"

I looked down. His jacket was unzipped, and his head was uncovered. In his small, bare, hands was clutched a dented, red truck.

It was rusty, and the tailgate was missing. His fingers stuck to the cold metal as he handed it to me. I saw, too, that his feet were bare inside his snow-filled shoes. He had walked at least a mile in the deep snow.

I picked him up and carried him into the building. His home room teacher met us in the hall. She took one look at him, scooped him into her arms and carried him to her room.

Moments later the bell rang, and I walked numbly to my classroom. I hung my coat over the back of my chair, sat down, and stared at the wall. I closed my eyes as tightly as I could, but once again I saw distinct images. I sat there for a long while trying to wipe away the tears, and the pictures of a small, black dog, and a rusty, red toy truck. ❄

A star of the past

By John B. Matheson Jr.

Y MOST MEMORABLE CHRISTMAS didn't occur when I was a boy amid the spine-tingling joys of electric trains, bicycles, baseball gloves and skates. Nor was it as a father seeing starry eyes of little children as they beheld the wonders of Christmas day.

Christmas of 1945 found me serving in the army of occupation in Frankfurt, Germany. The war had ended about seven months before, but most of the city was rubble. Many of the homes left unscathed were taken over for housing of the United State military. Three of us officers lived in a three-story house that easily would have served as home for three families.

Each weekday we would go to our office and return in the evening to find the beds made and the house spotlessly cleaned by an old German woman who was hired by the U.S. Army to be housekeeper for a number of houses in that area. Only occasionally would we see this frail, little lady as she busily engaged in her tasks. Our conversations were limited for she spoke no English and our German was poor, but through a sign language and smiles we indicated satisfaction with her work.

Weekly I went to the post exchange to get my ration of candy bars, soap and incidentals. Though I sometimes grumbled about the poor selection available I always purchased all I was allowed and put the excess in to my footlocker. As Christmas approached I thought I should give some gift to the housekeeper, so from my abundance of the footlocker I filled a large cardboard box with candy bars, soap and cans of fruit juice. In the system of barter among the Germans my gift to her was worth many, many dollars — but the cost to me was negligible.

Knowing she would not work on Christmas Day, as I left for the office on December 24th I placed on the table where it would be seen my gift box and a Christmas greeting. All day I felt rather smug as I thought of my generous gift. She would be like an heiress in the poverty of her neighborhood. How lucky she was. How beholden she would be to me, to the generous American. And yet my gift was not given in compassion — merely out of pity and for self satisfaction.

As I came home in the darkness of the December evening I saw the dim glow of the lamp filtering through the window. The house was still. My gift and the recipient were gone, but in the glow of that lamp I saw on the table her Christmas note and her gift to me. I had expected no gift, but there it was — all she could afford, and given in the spirit of Christmas.

I could imagine Frankfurt of years before with its bright shops and cheerful crowds. I could see the stately opera house and public buildings, the parks, the bridges. I could see the gaiety of days before the ravages of war when Frankfurt, her beloved city, was alive and vibrant.

But now Frankfurt was old and broken and the little housekeeper was old and frail.

What could a poor, little old lady give? She could give from her poverty and from her heart her fondest memories of her beloved city of yesteryear, and she could give the Christmas star.

On that dimly lit table along with her painstakingly written "Merry Christmas," were 10 old and dog-eared picture post card scenes of Frankfurt. She had placed each card on edge and fastened them together so that every two cards formed a point and all 10 together formed the Christmas star.

She had little to give, but it was all she had. Though 19 years have gone, her Christmas star is still a symbol to me of love and giving and of the first Christmas star of 19 centuries ago.

A gift from Jimmy

By Jettie J. Anderson

MY MOST MEMORABLE CHRISTMAS began when I mounted the steps of the Primary Children's Hospital in Salt Lake City. I glanced about thinking how miraculous it was that the gently falling snow could transform drab, somber buildings and leafless shrubs into a beautiful sparkling winter wonderland.

I could hear Christmas carols playing softly, and paused momentarily to enjoy "Silent Night, Holy Night." For to me, a great part of Christmas enjoyment is found in the music.

Stomping the snow from my boots, I entered the toasty warm foyer and stood admiring the beautifully decorated Christmas tree. I was glad I had said yes when the American Legion asked me to sing two numbers on the children's Christmas program.

Entering the auditorium I immediately was caught up in the spirit of the occasion. There were so many excited, wide-eyed youngsters! Some children were in wheelchairs, others wore heavy braces and still others were on crutches, but everyone was excited and stimulated by the magic that is Christmas.

From the first moment I was drawn to one particular little boy. He had a radiance about him that was difficult to describe — a radiance yet a pathetic quality. Perhaps it was his big brown eyes, set in a too-thin face, his beautiful wistful smile, or the heavy braces on both legs.

Part way through the program it was announced the children had a surprise for us. Each child presented members of the program with a little gift — a candy bar, a package of gum — everyone except Jimmy, that is.

Jimmy slid out of his wheelchair and slowly made his way over to me.

"Singing Lady," he said, "I didn't have any money to buy gifts, but I drew this picture of you while you sang."

As I accepted the picture, two other boys laughed at Jimmy. Tears welled in his eyes as he turned and made his way back to the wheelchair.

I could hardly wait for my next number; at last the time came.

"Thank you for all your gifts," I said, "but the gift I shall treasure always is this picture Jimmy drew. Bless you, Jimmy, for sharing your talent with me!"

Then I dedicated "Santa Claus is Coming to Town" just to Jimmy.

What a happy boy he was! His face beamed as he tapped out the rhythm against his wheelchair. He laughed merrily, and when I finished singing he blew me a kiss.

"Looks like you have made a conquest with Jimmy," one of the nurses whispered. "Isn't it too bad that he has less than two months to live."

Never has a statement shaken me like this one did.

I looked at Jimmy's angelic face and a lump rose in my throat. I knew if I talked to him again I would cry, so the minute our program ended I tried to skip out.

Suddenly a voice called out:

"Singing Lady, aren't you going to tell me goodbye?"

I swallowed the lump in my throat, and going over to him I smiled and said:

"You bet, Jimmy! Do you have a kiss for me before I leave?"

"Naw, men don't kiss, we shake hands." Then he extended a thin, white hand.

As I took his hand in both of mine, try as I would, the tears spilled over.

"Are you blubberin'?" Jimmy asked.

"No, not really, it's just that I am so happy over the picture you drew of me."

Jimmy glanced around hurriedly, then he whispered:

"Bend down."

As I bent down beside Jimmy he kissed my cheek, looking around quickly to make sure no one had seen that unmanly act.

I hugged him close, turned, then practically ran from the hospital.

As I stumbled out into the December night the cold wind made the tears running down my face feel like icicles. I wanted to shout the age-old question, "Why, why must these things happen?"

I asked the question, knowing full well the answer: *"Thy will, not mine, be done."*

Jimmy will always be the warm part of the Christmas I remember best.

A chocolate Christmas

By Richard R. Schaar

T WAS DURING THE WAR YEARS. We landed in New Guinea on Dec. 24th and it was raining and hot and muggy. Trucks took us 22 miles inland and oh! what a lonely, lost forsaken feeling we had — only jungle, heat, swamp and bugs. We pitched our tents and our only light was a piece of tent rope about 4 inches long stuck in a tin can of kerosene.

Already on board ship I struck up an acquaintance with a lonesome G.I. and we became fast buddies. His tent was next to mine.

I was unpacking my duffel bag and wondering what I could give him at least, for Christmas tomorrow. We each had the same G.I. equipment so there was nothing in that line to give him and beyond that there was nothing you could buy. But, I did remember seeing a scrawled sign on a tree back on the road that simply said, "PX." This I must investigate. I made an excuse to my buddy that I was going to look around a bit. Since trucks were coming and going all the time, it was no job to simply hang onto the sides of one and the fellows inside would pull you in.

The roads were bad so the trucks had to go slow anyway. I asked them about this PX and they said, "Well, they call it that for want of a better name — they don't have any PX supplies yet — just a few candy bars." They told me when to jump off and, sure enough, a few candy bars were all they had and all of them took up only the space inside the lid of a footlocker. A sign said: "Only one bar to a customer — Leave some for the others." All bars were 4 cents each. I picked out a Hershey milk chocolate bar and hitched a ride back to camp.

I took a piece of waxed-bread-wrapping paper that I found near the PX and wrapped the candy bar. At least the paper had some colored lettering on it from a San Francisco bread company. Then I took an empty ration can and put some fern leaves in it. I then took a piece of stationery and made a Christmas card out of it with some sketches of eight water buffaloes pulling an Army truck (representing Santa's reindeer and sled), added a serious four-line jingle I made up and then placed them all together on top of an ammunition box and thus my Christmas shopping was done. I covered it all with the end of my tent flap so my buddy couldn't see it.

Christmas morning came and I was already up — I couldn't sleep much anyway because my mind was across thousands of miles most of the night. I went to my buddy's tent and he also was up and puttering around. I wished him a Merry Christmas and told him Santa had come — to come over to my tent and take a look. I threw back the tent flap and he just stood there with tears in his eyes.

Finally he said to come back to his tent, because Santa had been there, too. We walked back and he threw back the cover of his bunk and there also was a Hershey milk bar and a homemade card. That is why he was puttering around when I came the first time. I almost choked with feelings. Then when he unwrapped my "present" and saw that we had each given the other the same thing we both just stood there and shook our heads and laughed and cried. I asked where he got it from and he said, "Well, do you remember that PX sign we passed back on the road as we were coming in . . . ? Well, after you took off yesterday . . . " and the rest he didn't have to tell me. We both had the same idea and did the same thing.

We sat down together and sparingly nibbled on our chocolate bars and talked about the folks at home and hoped next year things would be different.

So simple, but how can anyone forget it? ❄

Mrs. T's potbelly

By Mrs. Alma C. Nielson

WE SMILE WHEN WE REMEMBER the big black and silver dining room stove which played a great role in that long-ago, beloved Christmas Eve.

Our family called the stove Mrs. Thompson, and the name was said with love. How she got her name is now in the forgotten past, but Mrs. Thompson was warm and beautiful to our family.

Our mother, Mrs. Ruth Peay Farrer, a widow, lived in a tall house on West Center Street in Provo, Utah, with us children. There were Agnes, 13; Margretta, 11; Roger, 8; Leah Ruth, 5, and Berthelda, 2.

Roger had a talent and a passion for taking things apart. On the day before Christmas, 1921, he discovered that Mrs. Thompson could be undressed.

By removing a bolt or two and sliding some metal slots out of some matching grooves, we could take off the fancy, nickel-plated apron Mrs. Thompson wore across her front. Then we could take off the two ornate plates, hanging down either side of Mrs. Thompson's middle. The back of her black metal blouse was trimmmed with two smaller shining nickel plates. These also would come off without too much trouble.

Mother came to view the scene after Leah Ruth tattled on Roger.

"She certainly looks a fright, standing there undressed," Mother said. "I'll give you two minutes to dress Mrs. Thompson again."

In two minutes, Mrs. Thompson was reassembled into all her black and silver glory. As Mother watched, we could tell she was turning something over in her mind.

"This nickel plate is always nice and warm, but never too hot," she said as she patted Mrs. Thompson's trimmings, here and there.

"We have some of Berthelda's baby blankets. Suppose I said you may each take one of the warm plates upstairs to bed, wrapped in a blanket? Your beds would be warm in no time!"

Mother came up with a plan that evolved into a family tradition. "On winter days," she said, "the first one to get home and get the assigned chores done, gets to take off Mrs. Thompson's apron at bedtime. The next two will sleep with her sleeves and the last two may take the smaller plates from her back."

We all looked at Baby Berthelda, knowing full well that she could charm us out of any part of Mrs. Thompson's wardrobe she wanted — and get it carried upstairs besides.

Mother continued laying down rules for our newest tradition. "If Mrs. Thompson isn't quickly and properly dressed as soon as you are up in the mornings, there will be no more undressing her at night."

She was interrupted by a local merchant who came to the door with a big box.

"Some clothes for the children," he said, and walked away without seeming to hear our calls of "Merry Christmas!"

Mother's hands trembled as she untied the twine. There was smiling anticipation on her face. She was likely thinking of warm sweaters, gloves and long underwear.

For just a moment, when she lifted the cover, I thought I saw a look of dismay — but when she turned back to us, she was laughing. It was the exciting, musical laughter that bridged many perilous moments in our growing-up years.

"Such marvelous costumes for you to wear," she laughed as she held up a shopworm coat with leg-o-mutton sleeves. There was a window-faced bathrobe trimmed with feathers and ribbon rosebuds. Also two pairs of cracked riding boots, a hat with a bird's nest on top, plus a dozen other dusty items that couldn't be sold.

In the next few minutes, we remembered that Mother used to do a musical act with our father, before he died in the influenza epidemic of 1919. They had been offered a spot on the Pantages entertainment circuit, but turned it down as "no way to bring up the children."

Now, we caught a glimpse of how Mother must have looked, years before, as she floated across the stage in her red velvet gown and her big hat from Aunt Bertha's millinery store.

She was at her best on that Christmas Eve of 1921. We howled with delight as she pulled on a pair of the riding boots and topped them with the bathrobe and the bird nest hat. She went to the piano and we all gathered 'round, loving every minute, because we were a musical family. The neighbor children began flocking into the room as they always did when Mother or Agnes played the piano and I played the violin.

When it was almost dark, we bundled up and went out to the hay-scented barn for our favorite geography game.

Our father's old touring car didn't run anymore, but it was kept in the barn for us to use as we pretended to travel to the countries of the world. On Christmas Eve, we always traveled to Bethlehem.

Agnes took over the steering wheel. Roger twisted the old crank. I held the lantern.

Our imaginations led the way as Mother pointed out the shepherds' fields, the crowded inn and the stable where Baby Jesus was born. Neighbor children came inside the barn which was shared by the car, our cow and a winter supply of hay and grain. We all joined in singing "O Little Town of Bethlehem."

Soon it was time to climb the stairs, each carrying a part of Mrs. Thompson to warm ourselves from toes to sleepy eyes.

On Christmas morning, we hurried down from the attic with our respective parts of Mrs. Thompson's wardrobe. We put our clothes on her in a hurry.

When she was dressed, the magic of Christmas glowed around her. We lit the candles on the Christmas tree and as they sent up spears of amber light, Mrs. Thompson caught the glow and tossed it back to us from her apron and nickel-plated sleeves. She gathered us into a warm circle around her as Christmas fire glowed through her isinglass windows.

In our warm circle, we emptied oranges, bananas, nuts and candy from our long black stockings we'd hung the night before. We opened small homemade gifts. My favorite was from Mother — a tiny corn husk doll sleeping in a gilded milkweed pod.

Many Christmases have passed since them. Mother and Agnes have left us. The rest of us often ask each other. "Were we rich or poor?" and "Does anybody remember what became of Mrs. Thompson?"

Only a small part in the Christmas play

By Mavis H. Steadman

IT WAS MY FIRST YEAR teaching drama in junior high, and I was selecting students for the annual Christmas program. I was anxious to prove my ability as a new teacher and wanted only outstanding talented students in the show. Imagine my dismay when the first one to try out was Robert. He was the joke of the school, a small, mentally slow, misfit boy who always looked like an unmade bed. He was definitely not what I wanted, but he seemed so eager, that I decided to make him one of 30 choral scripture readers and hide him on the back row.

During the next weeks, Robert became my shadow. He was first to memorize his part and was always waiting by my door to practice. Each rehearsal seemed the most important thing in his life. It was his only chance to belong and do something special. Seeing his total dedication, the other students stopped laughing at him and regarded him with new respect. When it came time to choose one solo reader, I picked Robert, much to the astonishment of other teachers.

Knowing it would be impossible financially for students to buy costumes, I told each to bring an old white shirt, and I would dye them red, and we would make green ties. Robert came to me in tears.

"We don't have any old white shirts at our house," he said. "I have six brothers, and we just wear each other's. If I brought one, my little brothers wouldn't have anything to wear. Does this mean I can't be in the play?"

I assured him that since I had four sons I would look through my closets and find one he could wear. The next week I brought the 30 brilliantly dyed red shirts straight from my clothesline.

"Now take these home and have your mothers iron them for the dress rehearsal tomorrow. And be sure you look nice," I added firmly.

Minutes before dress rehearsal as I was nervously straightening crooked green ties, shouting light cues, and tracking down lost props, I saw Robert in his red dyed shirt, UNIRONED, just the way I had given it to him. Screaming my disapproval, I asked him why it hadn't been ironed. He explained that his mother had been taken to the hospital suddenly, and in all the confusion his sisters had forgotten about it, and he couldn't find the iron. I jerked him by the arm and pushed him to the Sewing Room, muttering all the way how he couldn't spoil the whole program with a wrinkled shirt.

I shall never forget his shame as I ordered him to take off his shirt so I could iron it. He unbuttoned it slowly, handed it to me and stood shrinking before me, and a class of giggling girls, in the dirtiest, ragged underwear I had ever seen. I quickly ironed the shirt, thrust it at him and marched him back to the auditorium.

The rehearsal went smoothly and Robert performed well as usual. I delivered my final directions to the cast.

"I want everyone in costume on stage tonight at seven o'clock. And don't be late. I don't want any last minute worries," I added, glaring at Robert.

Seven o'clock came. Most of the students were in their places — but no Robert. 7:15 came. All the students were in their places and most of the audience. But no Robert. I was wild. 7:25 came and still no Robert. In desperation, I told another student to read Robert's part so the show could go on. Just as the curtain opened at 7:30, I saw a rather pale, shaken Robert slip into his place. I sighed with relief, but vowed I would let him know the anxiety he had caused me.

Robert performed as if he were inspired. Never have I heard St. Luke given with such simple meaning and tenderness. He held the surprised audience spellbound. After the show I received congratulations from parents, but no one from Robert's family was there. When the crowd had gone, I found him waiting for me. I immediately unleashed my fury, telling him how worried I had been.

"Why were you so late?" I demanded.

He answered me softly. "Just as I was leaving the house, we got a phone call from the hospital. My mother died tonight. But I knew you were depending on me so I came as soon as I could."

The years have flown, but the lesson the drama teacher learned lingers. No matter how many Christmas programs I direct, the angel who proclaims *Peace On Earth, Good Will Toward Men*, for me, will always be an 8th grade misfit boy named Robert in a dyed red shirt. ❄

Christmas dolls

By Beatrice Tolman Gardner

IT WAS CHRISTMAS EVE, 1923. My husband, Roy, and I hadn't a cent to buy gifts for our little daughters, Elaine, 5, and Roa, 3.

It was impossible for a man to find work in Star Valley that winter. We had known for weeks that ours would be a meager Christmas.

The girls' last year's dolls were hidden away, gorgeous in outfits made from an old satin formal.

A small tree stood in the corner, not too resplendent, in colored paper chains and popcorn strings the little girls had spent many happy hours helping prepare.

At dusk my husband and I were feeling pretty despondent. There wasn't even candy for their stockings.

Then an old friend called in to pay $10 he had borrowed before we were married.

"I bet you thought I was never going to pay you," he said jovially.

"It couldn't have come at a better time," Roy answered with feeling.

He was hardly out of the door when Roy said, "Get on your things while I get a girl to stay with the children. We'll get that sugar and laundry soap and other stuff you've been wanting."

The night was cold. A blizzard hurled icy particles against our happy faces as we walked briskly toward town.

Beside candy I envisioned a few cheap ornaments for the tree. That $10 greenback seemed like a million dollars to us that night!

"Now don't go planning anything for me. I don't need anything!" He was beating his cold, wet hands together to keep them from freezing. My own hands were thrust deeply into the pockets of my shabby old coat. His coat was even more threadbare.

Didn't need anything! He needed everything! I had thought of a cheap pocketbook, but now it was warm woolen gloves I would buy him.

When we stopped to admire the display in Burton's store window, I said, "I'm glad we didn't bring the little girls. Their dollies wouldn't look like much in comparison." Then I looked at him suddenly. "You're not taking cold, are you?"

"No, it's just this dang wet snow." He thrust his handkerchief back into his pocket.

We walked on to the other store, Taysom's. Before going in, Roy had to feel the assurance of the bill in his pocket.

"It's gone!" he said. "I put it in this pocket under my handkerchief." He turned his pocket inside out; then all of his pockets inside out. It was gone!

We searched the ground at our feet every inch of the way back to Burton's. Once I thought I had found it, but it was just a snow encrusted green gum wrapper partially buried.

People passing along the dim street or going in and out of the store must have thought we were crazy, down on our knees frantically sifting through drifts with icy, numb fingers.

"I only hope someone finds it who needs it more than we do," I was crying.

"No one will ever find it after this blizzard," Roy said with conviction.

And no couple whose spirits had so recently soared ever walked home in deeper dejection.

"We promised the baby tender a quarter," I moaned. Then I thought of a dainty wool sweater I had bought while teaching school before my marriage. It was much too small for me now.

Delighted, the baby sitter ran home with it.

We were in each other's arms. The room was warm and cozy; plenty of wood to keep it that way.

"We're in no danger of starving. We have flour, elk meat and our own vegetables. Old Red will keep us in milk, cream and butter."

"The children are healthy and we have each other."

Next morning two happy little girls were admiring their dolls. "Mrs. Santa made these dresses," Elaine told her little sister with assurance. Then she called, "Mama, how did Santa get your pretty dress out of the big trunk?"

Their Daddy and I were laughing in the kitchen.

Often when we see our children and grandchildren rush from one expensive gift to another, unable to decide which is best, our minds go back to this, our most memorable Christmas.

A gift of friendship

By LaRue H. Soelberg

HIS CHRISTMAS HAD BEGUN like any other. The laughter of our happily excited children was evidence that Santa had indeed been able to decipher the hastily scrawled notes mailed weeks before.

As was our custom, LeRoy and I would wait until the children had sufficient time to inspect, test, compare and segregate their new treasures before we would open our gifts.

The similarity of this Christmas, to any other, ended here.

The loud knock on the front door demanded immediate answer.

"Come quick!" There was urgency in our friend's voice. "I think you have a fire at your store!"

Fears flooded my mind as I ran through the vacant lot to the store — a small grocery business, which was not yet half paid for.

There were no flames rising from the building, but the windows were solid black!

A fireman came running up and put his hand against the window.

"No heat!" he seemed relieved, "there's no fire now — let's open it up."

Our hopes were raised. Perhaps we had not lost everything!

He turned the key and pushed open the door. The dense, choking smoke that had filled every minute space of the small building drifted out into the street.

My heart sank! It was like looking at the inside of a coal-black furnace. Not a crack, not a corner, not one can stacked beneath another, had escaped the ugly black filth!

LeRoy, with the help of some of the firemen, removed the motor that had burned itself out. We stood gazing in disbelief at the result.

True, the store had not burned, but was it salvageable? Perhaps the building and equipment could be cleaned, but what about the thousands of bottles, cans and cartons? Even if they could be saved, how could we possibly survive the closing of business for even a few days?

"Only one thing to do," the voice was surprisingly cheerful. "Let's see if we can clean it up."

We were reluctant to accept this offer of help. After all, wasn't this Christmas? A day to be spent with family and loved ones.

"Come on," he joked, "my son will be glad to get me out of the house so that he can play with his electric train. Get me a bucket and some soap."

No sooner would we equip one volunteer with cleaning items, when another would appear at the door, demanding, as one neighbor put it, "A chance to participate in this joyful, holiday project."

Each person who came to the door uttered an astonished, "Oh, no!" and then, "Where do you want me to start?"

By 11 a.m. there were more than 40 people—friends, neighbors, firemen, patrons and new acquaintances, scrubbing away at the terrible black goo. Still they kept coming! We were overwhelmed!

The men had taken over the cleaning of the ceiling, the most stubborn and difficult task of all. The women were working in twos, taking items off the shelves, cleaning what they could and boxing the rest.

One young lad, who was recuperating from a broken leg, made trips to the cafe to get hamburgers and potato chips to feed the workers. Another brought turkey and rolls, which,

I'm certain, were to have been the biggest part of their Christmas dinner.

An energetic teenager must have run 20 miles emptying buckets and refilling them with clean hot water.

A service station operator brought hundreds of old cleaning rags.

An electrician worked on a motor replacement, and soon had the refrigerator case operating again.

This was no ordinary cleaning job. Every inch had to be scrubbed, scoured, washed and rinsed. Sometimes this procedure had to be repeated seven times before the white of the walls and ceiling would show through. Yet, everyone was laughing and joking, as though they were having a good time!

"Actually, I only dropped by to supervise," came a comment from behind the bread rack.

"I bet this cures you of following fire trucks," a fireman chided his wife.

We all laughed when an attractive blonde woman, who was perched on top of the vegetable case and now bore a striking resemblance to a chimney sweep, burst out with a chorus of "Chim Chim Cheree."

It was shortly after 2 a.m. when we locked the front door. Everyone had gone. As they finished their jobs, they just slipped out — not waiting for a word of thanks or a smile of appreciation.

We walked home hand in hand. Tears flowed freely down my cheeks. Not the tears of frustration and despair that had threatened earlier, but tears of love and gratitude. Business would open as usual tomorrow — because 54 kind people had the true spirit of Christmas in their hearts.

Our children had left the tree lights burning and our presents lay unopened in a neat pile on the floor. They would wait until morning. Whatever those gaily wrapped packages contained, would be dwarfed, indeed, by the great gift of friendship given to us that Christmas Day.

A surprise visitor
By Erin Parsons

N THE DAY BEFORE Christmas, Daddy brought home two things: a skinny pine tree and an equally skinny black kid named Greg.

"Greg will be spending Christmas with us," announced Daddy. "But Alan!" gasped Mother, "Christmas is tomorrow!" "I know," replied our puzzled father, "that's why I told you today."

Mother threw on her coat and raced downtown, trying to guess what a displaced New York youth would want for Christmas. In the record shop: "The Screaming Meemies? The Asthmatic Six?"

Daddy was a psychologist then at Job Corps, a program to train underprivileged youth. He had often brought home stray students, but the others had at least been friendly. Tym, the oldest, took Greg upstairs to the guest room. Greg clutched his shabby bag to his short and slender frame, listening to Tym's questions but seldom answering.

The rest of us turned to Daddy. "Why for Christmas?" we moaned, "Why him?" Instead of answering, he told us a story. Greg had lived on the streets of New York since his parents threw him out at eight. He joined a gang, fighting with them and stealing food and clothing. Now 16, this was to be his first Christmas. "He's uncomfortable around people he's had no experience with," Daddy explained, "but he's very aware of what's going on around him. Give him a chance, he'll respond." When Dad had finished, I felt a lump in my throat and a hard knot of guilt in my chest for not welcoming Greg immediately.

Our attention turned to the tree. Daddy had no trouble getting it through the door; it was paper-thin and had branches only on one side.

Daddy freely admitted that he had retrieved the pine after it fell off the back of a truck. "It'll be fine once we fluff it up," he confidently assured us. After 25 minutes of 'fluffing," it was clear that the tree would take up no more than a fraction of living room space.

I didn't dare laugh at the awful tree to its face; I was afraid of offending its dignity. We waited in the kitchen, out of earshot, to moan about its sagging branches and how it listed to one side.

Greg permitted no pity; he had a certain, fierce pride. He was quiet, not taking part in much of the friendly banter, but listening carefully. I occasionally caught his smile as we struggled to decorate the disastrous Christmas tree. He patiently tied on branches, and it was Greg who devised a prop of bricks to make it stand straight. When we were finished, he eyed it thoughtfully. "It's an ugly tree" he said. "Yes," I agreed. He grinned suddenly. "I like it."

At dinner, Greg didn't join in as all six of us children seized serving bowls. As always, he wouldn't ask for anything.

Christmas morning, Greg opened his hastily bought presents with the rest of us. He seemed to like the Screaming Meemies and wolfed an impressive quantity of Christmas dinner, even by the standards of our voracious teenage appetites.

After dinner, Mother found him a warm ski jacket to cover his ragged coat, and Daddy located a spare set of skis. On the slopes, Greg caught on to the movements quickly, snowplowing contentedly and waving as we shot past on our way to the bottom. On the ski lift, I looked wistfully at the thick pines and spruces, covered with snow and dotting the mountainside.

"Why couldn't Daddy have brought home a pretty tree?" I complained. Sister Tamara was more understanding. "Anyone can start with a fancy tree. Making one beautiful is better."

When we returned home, I examined our Christmas tree. Covered with popcorn strings and glass balls, it did seem a little taller and thicker.

At our Christmas program that night, Greg played a very credible Grinch in the play. The family was treated to another of his sudden grins as we applauded. And then Mother took out the Bible. She smoothed the worn cover. "Who'll read the Christmas story?" Greg reached out a hand. "I will." He began, his soft voice hesitant at first, then gaining strength. His strange Eastern accent spun the familiar words into timeless beauty. The firelight flickered on his chocolate skin as his hands turned the last page. We were all silent when Greg finished. As he shut the Bible, I glanced at our Christmas tree. The propping-up had worked; it stood tall and glittering in the corner.

Greg finished his training at Job Corps and moved out of Utah. In the years since, we have always gone to an expensive lot to pick out a thick spruce. But to me, none have every measured up to Greg's first Christmas tree. ❄

When out on the lawn...

By Ramona Stover

BOUT 12 YEARS AGO while my children were still young, we had occasion to live on a homestead one winter. We moved in October and stayed until school was out. Living conditions were primitive — kerosene lamp, wood heater, pump outside — at this little house nestled in the hills. Although my husband was out of work we had enough money for necessities, but no extras.

Around the first of December we had a talk with the children. We discussed the economic situation and decided one of them would hunt for a tree in the hills above us. I was to go to town and buy one present for each. However, the roads became impassable and I became also became ill at the time.

The weather got quite bad with rain and snow flurries. I got everyone to bed early each evening, and when everyone was tucked in, I read a few chapters from such books as "Swiss Family Robinson."

When the weather cleared a little, the oldest boy, then 13 years old, went out and found us a nice tree. We strung popcorn and made decorations out of pictures from magazines. Even the little ones helped, and the tree looked quite festive.

The two youngest were girls 3 and 4 years of age; four boys, 5, 8 10, 13, and then girls 14 and 16 years.

Ten days before Christmas it really started to snow; you know, those big, lazy flakes that really cover the ground. It snowed for a week and the weather cleared, then it froze hard. The temperature was 5 degrees above zero at night. By Christmas Eve the roads were impassable and my illness kept me in. There were no gifts under the tree for eight small children.

The children popped corn and ate apples while telling their favorite stories.

I looked out the window after the light was out and the children were snug in their bed. "What a beautiful Christmas Eve," I thought. The sky was clear and dark, stars twinkled like diamonds and they seemed closer then I had ever seen them. The full moon was almost bright enough to read by. Everything was so quiet and peaceful, the warmth of the crackling fire, and finally the heavy breathing of tired children. It was 10 o'clock and my husband and I decided to go to bed before the house got cold. I immediately dropped off to sleep.

Sometime later I awoke. A thrill shook me as I reached for my bathrobe. I heard the sound of sleigh bells on the frosty air. One by one the children awoke and were talking in hushed tones. The younger ones said it MUST be Santa's reindeer, while the older ones were quietly mystified with an awed look on their faces. Finally, we could see two figures racing right up to our door with sleigh bells ringing with every step now. There they lifted a large box off a sled and put it on the porch. With a hearty "Merry Christmas," they ran back the way they had come, without another sound.

By the time I got the door open and saw the big box bulging with all sizes of gaily wrapped packages, Santa's two helpers were well on their way home.

If we didn't have a time Christmas morning unwrapping presents! It was wonderful: games, mittens, candies, fruits, something swell for everyone including Mom and Dad. I think it was all the more wonderful because our Santa was a neighbor boy about 25 years old. It was his own idea and he had personally selected the gifts and paid for them. Then he wrapped and delivered them in this unique way with the help of one of his brothers.

We shall never forget this generous, thoughtful young man.

May God bless him and his family.

A Gift of Christmas

By Mrs. W. R. Swinyard

THE CHRISTMAS I REMEMBER BEST began with tragedy. It happened at six a.m. on one of those crisp Idaho Falls mornings the day before Christmas. Our neighbors, the Jessee Smith family slept peacefullly in their two-story home. The baby, barely six months old, was in a crib next to her parents' room, and three older children were upstairs.

Suddenly something jarred Jessee from his sleep. He thought he smelled smoke. Could a spark from the torch he'd defrosted the frozen winter pipes with the day before have started a fire in the basement? Still half asleep, he stumbled to the bedroom door and flung it open. Clouds of black smoke poured into the room. "Lorraine!" he yelled, "get the baby!" and ran toward the stairs and his sleeping children. The smoke was thicker as he gasped for breath. "Rick! Tom! Wake!" The boys scrambled out of their beds. "Run, boys!" Tom grabbed his younger brother's hand and they raced down the smoke-filled stairway to safety. His daughter's room was next. As Jessee groped through the heavy shroud of grey, he called, "Cindy! Cindy! Where are you?"

"Here Daddy, here!" He followed the frightened cries, scooped up his daughter in his arms, and with his hand over her face, felt his way out the room and down through a narrow path of searing flames. They coughed, choked, gasped for breath, until they at last stumbled out the door where a relieved wife and three children stood shivering in the snow.

Now the family looked to the smoke and flames pouring out the roof of their home — the home that the night before had held all their earthly treasures. It has also held a promise of Christmas, cider, homemade candy, and stockings waiting to be filled. They stood huddled in their nightclothes, barefoot in the biting cold and watched their Christmas burn up along with their house.

The spell was broken by the sound of sirens piercing the icy air. Firemen leaped from the huge red trucks and turned their powerful hoses onto the blaze. Seconds later, the bishop of the Smith's ward drove up, bundled the family into his car and took them to a home the ward elders' quorum had just completed as a fund raising project. They were not to witness the firemen's hopeless battle with the flames. For when the trucks finally pulled away, this time in silence, nothing stood of their house but its charred skeleton against the sky.

And tomorrow was Christmas! At our house we were putting the last secret wrappings on the presents, making the last batch of popcorn for popcorn balls to go in our Christmas stockings. We three children were attempting dubious harmony with our favorite carols and breaking into giggles at the results.

Then Dad came in with the news. We sat with serious faces listening to him tell of the fire, the narrow escape, the house where the Smiths were spending Christmas Eve.

Why? Mother said. Why did this happen, just at Christmas? It isn't fair. They had children, just the same ages as ours, she said. Jessee and Dad were the closest friends; they even joked that they were so close they wore the same size shirt. The same size shirt! "Bill," mother began hesitantly, "would you mind terribly if we gave Jessee one of the shirts I bought you for Christmas? You wear the same size . . . . " A hush fell on us all. We all seemed to be thinking the exact thing. "I've got it!" my ten-year old brother shouted out. "We'll give the Smiths a Christmas! A Christmas for Christmas!"
"Where could we get one?" my inquisitive little sister asked.
"We'll give them ours," the others chorused in.

"Of course! We'll give them ours!" The house rang with excited voices, until Dad's stern command silenced us. "Hold it! Let's make sure we all want to do this. Let's take a vote. All in favor, say aye."

"AYE!" chorused back at him. "Any opposed?" was met with silence.

The hours that followed are ones we will never forget. First we sat around the tree and handed out presents. Instead of opening them, the giver would divulge their contents so the label could be changed to the appropriate Smith family member. My heart fell when Dad handed Kevin a box wrapped in gold foil and green ribbon. "It's a baseball glove, son," Dad told him, and a flash of disappointment crossed Kevin's face. I knew how he'd longed for that glove, and Dad wanted to say, "You keep it, son," but he smiled as if he'd read our thoughts. "Thanks, Dad. It's just what Stan wanted, too," Kevin replied.

"Look, here's the recipe holder I made for you, that is, for Sister Smith." We signed all the tags, "FROM SANTA," and the activity that followed would have put his workshop elves to shame.

They had presents, but what about a Christmas dinner? The turkey was cooked, pies baked, the carrots and celery prepared, then all packed in a box. The Christmas stockings must be stuffed! Dad got a length of clothesline and some clothespins to hang the stockings with, but what about a tree? We looked at ours. Could we really part with it? "I know," Dad volunteered, "Let's decorate it with things they'll need." And so more things were added to the tree: a tube of toothpaste tied with red ribbon, a razor, comb, bars of soap nestled in the branches. Finally it was all ready.

It was a strange procession that silently paraded through the dark streets of Idaho Falls that night. Father led the way carrying a completely decorated tree. Mother followed with a complete Christmas dinner, down to the last dish of cranberry sauce. The three of us children pulled wagons and a sled piled with boxes of gifts. We waited until the last light was out in the Smiths borrowed home, then Mom and Dad stealthily carried each item in the door. When the last stocking had been hung, we turned again toward home.

All the way home I worried about what waited for my family at home. What if the others are disappointed? All that's left are a few pine needles and paper scraps. I couldn't have been more wrong. The minute we were back inside we were more excited than ever. Every pine needle and paper scrap was a reminder of the magic of the evening and we hadn't taken that to the Smiths. It was in our home as real as if you could see it.

A happier family never went to bed on a Christmas Eve, and the next morning the magic was still there. For our celebration we wrote a promise to each person on a card and presented it around a spruce branch tied in a red ribbon.

"One shoe shine. To Father. Love Kevin." "This is good for two turns doing the evening dishes. Love, your husband, Bill." And so it went.

Our Christmas dinner consisted of scrambled eggs and bacon, toast and sliced oranges. Somehow, I don't remember a better one. And I know we sang our carols that night with the same unconventional harmony, but they sounded sweeter than angels to me.

"Oh, mommy," said my small sister as she snuggled up for her bedtime Christmas story, "I like to give Christmases away." Tears blurred the book in mother's hands, because she knew that none of us would ever forget this Christmas; the one when we gave our best gift. As she read the story of the Baby born in a manger, it seemed our gift was but a small tribute to Him who gave his best gift, His Son to us.

Boxes full of love

By Hope M. Williams

THE FRAGRANT "MOUNTAIN" ODOR of the pinon pine Christmas tree; the soft white snow that lay in stillness around our farm home; the frosty window panes with their dainty patterns; the spicy goodness of frying doughnuts; the Christmas carols being sung everywhere; and the thrill of hearing St. Luke's story of the Saviour's birth, "And there were shepherds — " these were all part of the Christmas spirit, which as a child I had called my "good feeling," and now whenever I experience these things again, I start remembering . . .

Many of our Christmases then were very meager, and the things that are considered musts in most homes today were absent from our festivities, but the "feeling" was always so much present in our home that I never remember feeling too disappointed when "hoped for" things did not materialize.

The Christmas that comes most vividly to my mind was one of those meager ones. My twin sister, June, and I were about 10 years old, I think, and were painfully aware that Christmas gifts this year would be few. We were too young to know the real concern as our parents and older sisters did, but there seemed to be less gaiety than usual this year, and we felt it keenly.

So, in our eagerness to keep this happy "feeling," and because we had no money with which to buy gifts, June and I thought it would be fun to pretend we had a nice gift for Mother.

We wrapped up an empty small box, placed it in another empty box, then that one in another and so on, until we had quite a big box; then we wrapped it in green paper and tied it with a big wide red ribbon. It was the first package to be placed under the tree.

We were very pleased at first when Mother showed such interest in it, but when she keep looking at it and saying "ah—hmm?" in that cute way of hers, the closer it came to Christmas, the more we wished that we had something—just something—in it. We even lay awake at night whispering and wishing we could think of something really wonderful to put in that box! Finally we came up with the idea of putting a letter in it— a special one for her from us.

Christmas morning finally came, and Mother was still so curious about the package that my heart sank and I wished heartily that we had never thought of such an idea. When she asked to open the big package first, I was more miserable than ever.

June was miserable too, because she kept saying over and over, "It's really nothing, Mama," but Mother kept peeling off paper and raising her eyes in question as each box only proved to be outside another one.

"We were just fixing a kind of surprise," I said, miserably.

"My! Just look at this! Another box to open?" said Mother, with a smile on her face as more wrappings came off.

My pain was so acute by then that I remember trying to grab the box, tear the rest of the wrappings off and get it over with, but everyone kept saying, "Leave her alone, it's her gift," and "don't be so rude," mistaking my misery for my eagerness to have mother see what we had given her.

As the last box was unwrapped and the lid lifted off, I uttered one final plea, "We wish it were something really good, Mama."

There in the bottom of the last small box lay a folded piece of paper on which was written:

"Dear Mama,

We don't have a present to give you, but we are going to try to be better girls so you won't have to feel bad when you scold us and everything.

Love,

Hope and June."

Mother looked up from the paper with tears in her eyes, and with a dear sweet look on her face she said, "That's the nicest gift my girls could ever give me."

I have had the feeling ever since that no gift, no matter how costly, could ever be quite wonderful enough for such a mother!"

Wartime Christmas

By Mrs. Sije Terpstra

CHRISTMAS 1944 IN THE Netherlands, I never can forget! To be four years occupied by "das Herrenfolk," worked out in a terrible way! There was no food, heat, fuel, power, shoes, soap, insufficient clothing, and bedding. There was fear all around, killing going on all the time. No rest at day or night, for Hitler's spies and murderers were always around.

The Allied bombers were flying to destroy Hitler's system and property. Too many times in flights they had to unload their bombs above our heads. Our surroundings were often the target of the planes. There was no transportation in any way to visit friends, family, even if you might have had the spirit to do so. Life was to live from one hour to another. Birthday and other parties seemed to be of ancient times. Since a long time the stores were empty. No merchandise could be obtained. What there was were things brought in by people to try to trade them for the most needed things.

Life was hard and only to bear by them who had enough faith, ideals to go on. Ten thousands of friends, family, loved ones were already murdered by the Germans, sent to labor and concentration camps. And there in the biggest slaughter of all times, misery all over, was Christmas coming. . .

What a taunt, object of mockery to talk, think about Christmas. Primarily was there one thought, stay alive, survive! Don't surrender. But Christ's peace, reconcilable seemed not of this time. . . What to do? How could we make an occasion to celebrate Christmas? You almost could not, sometimes it was impossible to bear more. But those were only moments of thoughts. Afterwards the cry to live, survive was bigger. In our hearts we knew Hitler had to lose. The wicked would be destroyed. Good has always won over bad. So with these feelings, under these circumstances, we had to face Christmas. . .

For sheets I traded some sugar, cocoa, made candy of it. For some pitcoal stolen from the army of occupation, as penalty the death or concentration camp, we obtained some candles. By trading my shoes I got flannel, and could sew my little girl some pajamas. Thread to sew I got for milk, which I had traded on a farm. From leftovers of my sewing drawer I made my baby boy dolls. With their embroidered faces, they were real nice. Then came Christmas Eve. . .

For that occasion we lit the stove, put the candles on, some red paper around it. The kids got their candy, were very excited about it. Since long they had lost the taste of it. We had warm chocolate milk, and for half an hour we were singing Christmas songs, telling a Christmas story. It seemed to be a real Christmas. . .

No engines of planes were heard. The Allies did not fly. The Occupied Army celebrated their "Weinachten." Then we had to stop singing, telling a story. It was a too great luxury to have candles and stove on—we needed them for harder times. We had to lay down, all the beds put together in the living room. Trunks were packed for each of us, as we might have to flee, and children would be separated from their parents.

Sandbags were high piled up, outside of the window. We had to stay close together, every moment of destroying could be there. We went to bed, but slept with one eye and ear open for the coming air raids, Grune Polizei, or S.S. Nobody was safe. Especially not when you tried to be a good patriot, tried to fight the Germans. . .

But that Christmas we were happy! We were as a family alive! But that Christmas we knew what a value FREEDOM had. At that time had we known that 12 years later we would celebrate Christmas in free America, we could not have believed it. America, the greatest of all the Allies. Indeed land of freedom—promised land. . . That time a call of many weary hearts.

That this country always may stay free, in a free world, a world where Christ will be worshipped, I pray with all my heart. ✳

Dreams go up in smoke

By Richard Menzies

WHEN I WAS A KID, Christmas was a time of many improbable events, an age of belief marked not only by an unshakable faith in Santa Claus but in other strange and magical phenomena as well. The season of miracles began about a month before Christmas Day, ushered in by the appearance on our doorstep of a new Sears and Roebuck Christmas catalog, and until my 6th or 7th year I remained firm in the conviction that it had been delivered by elves.

After several days of more or less nonstop perusal of the toy section, my selection was made, and Mother, acting as Santa's secretary, would write down my order. Not on the handy Sears mail order form, but on a plain sheet of paper, which was then ceremoniously dropped into the roaring bowels of the coal furnace that glowed like a small Bessemer converter in our basement. The elves, she explained, would read my message in the smoke and forward it directly to Santa Claus at the North Pole, thus bypassing Sears middlemen in Chicago and saving a three-cent postage stamp by the way.

As my dreams went up in smoke, I would settle back uneasily to count the interminable days until Christmas Eve, when Santa, toting my 900-piece Buck Rogers Asteroid Space Base, would descend the chimney, somehow miraculously alighting into our living room and not the furnace.

It was a long wait, eons compared with today's brief holiday countdown, and with little to relieve the tedium save the third magical event of the season: the building of the Christmas tree.

Persons not of my immediate family tend to raise eyebrows at the mention of building Christmas trees, as if the custom were somehow peculiar. I suppose it's because so many have grown up in an age of storebought trees, of plastic ponderosa complete with rubber shrubbery and evergreen spray scent. Or perhaps they hark back to an earlier day when everyone lived on Currier and Ives farm, with a convenient sapling always growing within easy sledding distance. But at our house we had neither; as far back as I can remember, my father had always built our Christmas trees by hand.

Exactly where the custom originated I can't say, but I suspect it dates back to the Great Depression, when as a young man my father had worked as a carpenter for the Works Progress Administration. Like others of his generation, Dad had learned the hard way the value of a dollar, and this, combined with his woodworking skills and frugal Scottish genes, had steered him naturally into the business of tree building.

Mind you, he never learned to make a tree from scratch, although several times he came precariously close to it. For raw materials he'd shop the neighborhood tree farm, a make believe forest of ready-cut pines set up in a parking lot downtown. I suspect his original intention was to buy a decent tree, but as soon as the salesman quoted a price, visions of hard times immediately sprung to mind, the piped-in Christmas carols faded, replaced in his mind's ear by the skirt of ancestral bagpipes. Dad would stroll down the rows of second and third rate trees, kicking a trunk here, inspecting a price tag there, until at last he found one that answered to the tune of reasonable.

Usually it was a pretty sad looking tree, shopworn and loplimbed — hardly fit for kindling. One was so squat it looked like a fence post taken root, another so spindly it resembled a flagpole with a five o'clock shadow. And whenever he brought such a prize home, he was inevitable greeted with a concerted moan from wife and kids. But Dad said not to worry, and dragging the thing to his basement workshop, set to work with hammer and saw.

Anxious hours would pass as Dad worked on into the night. Upstairs, Mom and kids unpacked the ornaments and strung garlands of popcorn and cranberries, while downstairs Dad pruned and grafted and splinted broken limbs, rearranging them along the trunk in perfect geometrical order. When at last the hammering and sawing ceased, there was an expectant hush as we listened to footsteps ascending the cellar stairs. Then hailed by a chorus of hurrahs Dad would appear, cradled in his arms a beautiful born-again Christmas Tree.

Come Christmas morning, the man-made tree would shelter Santa's gifts, direct from Sears Roebuck of Alaska. I remember that my Christmas wishes always came true — I know now — thanks to the money my father saved by making his own trees and what my mother saved by incinerating our correspondence. But most of all I remember those trees, magnificent specimens of the kind that once inspired Joyce Kilmer's immortal couplet: "Poems are made by fools like me, but only God can make a tree."

My father was no fool, and I don't recall that he ever wrote a poem. But he always did make wonderful trees.

My unloved doll

By Annie Atkin Tanner

CHRISTMAS IS A TIME for memories: each one of us has a memory that is as sweet as the fragrance that comes from the pine scented candle that glows on the mantle-piece on Christmas Eve. The beauty of the candlelight brings back thoughts of other Christmas Eves and of a home that lives now only in memories.

My early Christmas memories are not of snow or tinsel of Christmas trees. We lived in a semi-desert, where evergreens would not tolerate the arid heat of summer, and they grew so far away that few of us every saw a spruce or a fir tree, and snow seldom fell.

As a child I never saw a sled, only in pictures. I never heard a sleighbell ring: I never wondered how Sants Claus could travel without reindeer. I only knew that he would come to fill our stockings.

My memories are of blue sky glittering with silver stars, and copper-colored moon making the night light strangely beautiful. Always beside the moon was the bright, golden, evening star twinkling in the frosty air. I always believed it was the Star of Bethlehem.

I remember frost-encrusted grass sparkling in the moonlight and changing the sidewalk into a diamond path that only children dream about. On many Christmas Eves, I walked along this jewelled way and heard sweet, young voices somewhere in the distance singing, "Silent Night, Holy Night;" and the night was holy to a child who thought that the angels could not have sung more beautifully on that other night so long ago.

On such a Christmas Eve as this, I remember my young mother with her three little girls sitting in front of the fireplace where a pitch log sent out its orange warmth. I recall the Christmas stories our mother read to us and of our shedding tears as she recited the sad story of "Annie and Willie's Prayer."

I have a picture in my memory of Mama playing the organ and three little girls with long braids standing around her, and of all of us singing, "Loud the Christmas Bells are Ringing," and "The Drifting Snow Lay in Wreaths of Pearly Whiteness on the Earth Below." It didn't make any difference to us that there was no snow outside and that the moonlight was making lovely patterns on the rose leaves and the honeysuckle that were still green.

The fact that our mother must have been very lonely didn't bother us at all. None of us could remember our father, who was only twenty-seven when he had died a few years before. She never let us feel her loneliness on Christmas Eve.

After we had finished our singing, we hung Mama's long, black stockings on the mantel-piece. We knew our own would not hold our dolls. This job done, we knelt by our mother's rocking chair to ask for sweet sleep and safety and to beseech Santa Claus, for the last time, to bring us the things we wanted so much.

This Christmas, I had prayed each night that Santa Claus would bring me a doll with real hair. I also had been a good girl longer than ever before, and so I was sure I would be rewarded.

My sisters and I were now ready for bed; as we turned the covers down the moon hung low over the Black Hills of my valley and shone pale gold over our bed. Its benediction brought peace and sleep to three tired, little girls.

In the blue dawning of Christmas morning I was awakened by the crackling sound of the good-smelling pine burning in the fireplace. Mama always made us get dressed before leaving our bedroom so I hurried into my clothes and ran to the fireplace. My heart seemed like it would burst with joy, for, looking out of the top of my stocking was the very doll I had prayed for, golden curls, blue eyes, pink dress and tiny black slippers. I held her in my arms and squeezed her with a love I have long remembered.

Soon the neighborhood kids came around and we showed each other our gifts. No one's doll seemed as lovely to me as mine did.

Soon after breakfast we began to get out hair combed and all "cleaned up" to go to Aunt Zaidee's for Christmas dinner. We were almost ready to leave, when my Uncle Joe called to wish us a "Merry Christmas." I immediately ran upstairs to get my doll to show him. I placed her in the fragile box she came in and started down the stairs. Just as I reached the bottom step, I stumbled and fell. The box crashed to the floor and my precious doll's head was broken into many, many small pieces. I gave a scream of anguish and the family, including my uncle, all rushed into the hall to see what had happened. There I was, tears falling and the golden curls, all that was left of my doll's head, clutched in my hand. The family tried to comfort me, but I wept on until, like a clock unwinding, I finally wore down.

After Christmas, my mother took the china head off my last year's doll and glued it on the kid body of my new doll. This was small comfort to me. The painted, yellow curls, pale blue eyes, the red, red mouth, could not take away my sorrow.

I never did learn to love that doll. Sometimes, I fancied she looked up reproachfully at me with her pale, China-blue eyes. I sometimes felt a tinge of sadness for my unloved doll, for how could last year's Rosie know that she could never take the place of my shattered dream doll?

Silent Night in the wind

By Rheauma West

IT WAS CHRISTMAS! It happened nearly fifty years ago, but what an impact on my memory. My Dad is one in a million, but that Christmas he was one in a universe.

There we were, seven of us children, anticipating our Christmas Eve social. It was held annually in our little community. We were chattering and laughing incoherently even though this was our first Christmas without Mama — and money.

As my Dad helped us button our coats my heart was singing. His was breaking. But his smile was deceiving. How well I remember him tenderly placing us on our long, homemade sleigh and pulling us to the church about a mile away. I remember him marching straight ahead with his shoulders back and chin up — I know now he was stepping off into something that took a lot of courage. As grown-ups, we draw on these memories as a source of strength. It was snowing. How warm and good it felt on our faces. We held tight to each other and above the crunch of snow beneath Father's feet, we could hear him softly whistling "Silent Night." Like magic, my unglued world was coming together.

How could a girl, 9, spilling with Christmas delight possibly know the inner turmoil my care-worn Dad was silently suffering. Mama had gone to the Great Beyond that previous summer. She had been confined to her bed for three years. We were poor, so Dad had assumed all father-mother responsibilities, as well as being Mama's nurse. He would leave his blacksmith shop hourly to check on her and us kids. His patience and love for Mama was a beacon of inspiration to us. Many times I saw him affectionately carrying her in his strong arms.

I remember his standing me on a stool by our big round kitchen table and teaching me to mix bread. I also learned how to turn the handle of our old wooden churn, while anticipating the miracle that was always performed inside. I got quiet professional at working the butter with the old wooden paddle, then pressing it into the pound mold. He taught me many household duties, but none are as vivid as helping Mama. I was her feet. I carted her food and water and helped her bathe. I delivered handmade gifts all over the community — from Mama. I don't think she ever missed a birthday, a wedding, nor a new baby. Then came that June day, her birthday, when God gave her the blessed gift of relief. My Dad was left to keep us alive physically, mentally and spiritually.

In August following Mama's death came our big fire. Our barns, sheds, straw and hay stacks as well as our livestock were caught in the path of the fiery destruction leaving only a charred, smoldering heap. Fear and horror raced through my veins, but the most indelible part of all was my Dad. While his world was crumbling to ashes, he was trying to rescue ours. He had a way of calming the tempest.

Now Christmas was upon him. We weren't even aware of how poor we were — nor of his Gethsemane. I felt his superior strength that night as he pulled the sleigh carrying his precious cargo.

The only thing I remember about the social was all the children clammering to tell Santa what they wanted for Christmas. But the sleigh ride was an imprinted memory. It was a special therapy that brought a kind of peace I hadn't known for years.

Later, in our front room around our pot-bellied stove Dad served us warm milk and bread. Our little Christmas tree, brought from the nearby hills, adorned one corner. Strings of our home-raised popcorn made it the most beautiful tree I had ever seen — or smelled.

Then Dad told us he was ready to give us our Christmas gift. We thought he should wait until morning, but he in his wisdom knew now was the time. We sat in wonderment. Seven of us waiting for Dad's gift.

Then he started talking. His gift flowed freely and clearly from his lips. He told us how much he loved us and how much we meant to him. Then he told us the story of the Christ Child. Never have I heard such a story! He brought it to life! He gave it purpose and meaning. Why Webster couldn't define the beauty of the gift he planted in our hearts that night. That gift of love, gratitude and peace is still mine. The light and warmth of the room was curiously powerful. We felt Mama's presence. We learned that loving someone was far more important than having something. I knew the true meaning of Christmas! We knelt together in a most humble family prayer and we thanked God for his gift to us — the Saviour of our world. Outside the world was singing "Silent Night" as our Dad tucked us into bed.

Christmas Day was a most special day. Dad had made us each a little gift and hung it on our tree while we slept. Our Christmas dinner consisted of home-cured bacon and milk gravy. Dad had a way of making a one dish meal taste like a seven course dinner. Our happiness knew no bounds. Many times since, my memory has been my Bethlehem Star. I have heard "Silent Night" in the wind and have smelled bacon while my turkey was cooking. But best of all —an occasional glimpse of Christ shining in my ninety-year-old father's face.

A timeless Christmas

By Ferenc Molnar

HE CHRISTMAS I REMEMBER BEST was a Christmas that we never had, but yet it was a Christmas that turned the world upside down for our family.

We will never forget that Christmas 20 years ago . . . a Christmas that came in the aftermath of the nightmarish and death-filled Hungarian revolution.

Life had been good for me, my wife Sarolta and our two daughters following World War II. I had formed a painting firm employing 35 painters in the beautiful town of Gyor. Then in 1949, with a mixture of terrorism, murder and fear, the Communists took over Hungary. They took away my business and the businesses of my friends and associates. We had to work as construction laborers to survive.

Communist secret police seemed to be everywhere. Many of our friends and acquaintances were taken away in the night, never to be seen or heard from again.

The oppression of the Communists finally crossed the brink of human patience and the people of Hungary revolted. Many of us took part. I went on the radio in my hometown and voiced my objections to the Communists.

The uprising was short lived. Russian Army tanks rolled into Hungary and silenced the revolt. Hundreds of thousands died. Many tried to escape and were killed.

After order had been restored, the Communists went about systematically liquidating those who had offended them.

On Christmas Eve, 1956, I went downtown in Gyor to buy my two daughters, 10 and 12, a present. I purchased two beautiful gold wristwatches. No matter how bad the times, Christmas still meant a great deal to us. I was so proud of the watches, I couldn't wait to give them to the girls.

I left the shop and was walking along, thinking about Christmas Eve, when I saw a face from the past. It was an old comrade of mine with whom I had served in World War II.

He seemed to be waiting for me. He said, "You must get away. I have been given orders to arrest you."

He said he had become a member of the secret police. "I will say I couldn't find you," he said. "But you must go now, this instant. Do you understand?"

I could only nod my head, yes. I was struck dumb. I had expected some retribution from the Communists. In fact, I was surprised that it had not come before. But one does not realize the enormity of Communist terrorism until it actually touches you.

I thanked my old friend and quietly walked away down the snow covered street pulling my coat around me. I had never been so cold in my life.

I had only a little money in my pocket. I went to a transport station and arranged for a ride west, to a town between Gyor and the Austrian border. I had thought about what I would do if this ever happened. I had a plan in the back of my mind.

The car took me to Dunaszeg. I got out, found a telephone and called my wife. Sarolta was in the middle of getting ready for Christmas Eve. She had baked breads, pies and cookies. My daughters were in their pajamas ready for bed. I told my wife what had happened and gave her instructions.

Sarolta and the children gathered up a few belongings. Then they dressed warmly and left the house. All that we had worked for was left behind.

They were able to get a bus and arrived in Dunaszeg about 10 p.m., Christmas Eve. The Austrian border was still 24 miles further west. But we could not go by bus. The roads to the west were well guarded.

We would have to get off the roads, walk across the snow-covered fields to the border and beyond, to Andau, a village I knew in Austria near the border.

As we set off, we could hear the church bells of the city ringing merrily. A loud speaker in the downtown area was playing Christmas songs.

We were cold, hungry and frightened. We had no idea how our journey would end. I knew there were mine fields near the border. And there were army patrols everywhere. We could not see any soldiers as we made our way through the snow, but we could see their flares shoot high in the air to illuminate the countryside.

Every time we saw a flare go up we would fall down in the snow to keep from being seen and wait until the dark night poured over us again. Then we would continue on.

We walked for hours. I never knew when we came to the border. There was no fence. Suddenly I saw soldiers. We hid. Then I could hear them. They were Austrian. We were safe in Andau. It was Christmas morning.

We were told there were American refugee camps in Salzburg. If we could get there, there might be a way for us to get to America. But we had few valuables.

Then I remembereed. I took out the two watches I had bought my daughters and showed them their presents. We agreed we would sell the watches to buy train tickets to Salzburg. I promised them both I would replace their presents as soon as I could.

We finally reached Salzburg. After a few months we were taken to America, arriving in Salt Lake City in March 1957.

I have been lucky. I have more painting business than I can handle. We have a nice home. Both my daughters are married. My wife and I have five grandchildren. We are all very happy here.

And yes, I gave my daughters gold wristwatches on their first Christmas in America.

Our Christmas this year will be filled with music and good fellowship and presents. Sarolta and I, and our daughters, will think about that long night 20 years ago — the night we missed Christmas.

The Spirit of Christmas

By Arnold E. Brady

HRISTMAS 1961 DID NOT hold much promise for happiness. My beloved wife had died in June and we were never blessed with children. Indeed, I was a hurt and lonely person sorrowing the loss of a loved companion.

My wonderful Christmas experience began on Tuesday, Dec. 19, with a telephone call and a young feminine voice filled with life and love and hope telling me, "This is the First Day of Christmas. Look on your front porch and you shall see what you shall see."

At the door I found a chocolate box decorated in holiday wrappings and filled with homemade fudge topped with walnuts. Each piece was carefully wrapped in foil.

The next evening I answered the telephone and again a young woman's voice said, "Sorry we missed you when we called earlier, but this is the Second Day of Christmas. Look out of your front door and you shall see what you shall see."

"Wait a minute," I said. "Who is this speaking?"

She answered, "Why the Spirit of Christmas." Then she hung up before I could say another word.

Going to the door I found a little tree about 18 inches high fashioned from a small branch in a can that was wrapped in tissue and tied with a ribbon. It was loaded with an assortment of nuts and an orange to keep the tree from falling over. The tree itself was decorated with nuts, popcorn balls wrapped in foil, candies, ribbons and tinsel.

Thursday night I hoped to catch a glimpse of the bearer of gifts by peeking from the edge of the window blind, but I saw no one. Watching the holiday program on television, I fell asleep. I was awakened by the telephone and the "Spirit of Christmas." Going to the front door I saw a small decorated box with a note which read, "Third Day of Christmas — Our gifts are small, it's true, but the wish of a Merry Christmas with them is brought to you." Yes, it was signed by "Christmas Spirit."

Grieving to share with my dear one the pleasure of this little gift, I placed it with the others — unopened.

Friday evening I peeked outside, hoping to see who brought these gifts. Again I fell asleep and again I was awakened by the Spirit of Christmas on the telephone. I was instructed to "look outside and see what is there on the Fourth Day of Christmas." This package I placed with the others — unopened.

Saturday was a clear, moonlit evening. I watched from the edge of the blinds for quite some time. Then I became engrossed in reading the evening newspaper. The telephone rang —"This is the Fifth Day of Christmas."

Greetings were exchanged, and then I asked, "Will I learn your identity?"

She replied, "I think not." Looking out I saw a package containing a lemon pie with that good homemade taste.

Opening the gift I received on the Third Day of Christmas when my niece came to my home I found it was a variety of homemade Christmas cookies. There were a Christmas star, snowman, reindeer, Christmas tree, a jolly fat man and a cookie candle to brighten the season.

The Fourth Day of Christmas package contained mixed nuts and some of the walnuts were individually colored red, green, white and yellow. I still have some of the cookies and nuts to cherish the sentiment and goodness they brought.

On Christmas Eve the Spirit of Christmas telephoned and said, "Our gifts are small, it's true, but tonight we have the best gift of all for you. We wish you health and happiness, good will and love from the Christmas Spirits everywhere.

God bless you Christmas Spirits wherever you are for such unselfish giving without thought of reward. With the other lovely and endearing recollections it brings, this is the Christmas I remember best. ❄

Freckle cream Christmas

By J. Stanford Staheli

BY THE TIME I WAS 10 YEARS OLD I HAD accumulated an over abundant supply of freckles from working and playing in the hot summer sun. These, along with a mop of unruly red hair atop my head, were a constant source of embarrassment to me. Though they came from well-meaning, friendly people, remarks such as "Hi, Spec!" kept me keenly aware of my homely appearance to others.

I dreaded meeting new people or relatives who weren't accustomed to my freckles and bright red hair. So, whenever newcomers appeared at our front door, I headed out the back and hid in an underground hut or in the old dilapidated Jewett that was parked under the shed in the far corner of the corral.

There I would stay until the all-clear signal was given by my handsome, dark-haired older brother, Ken. The last thing I wanted to hear was the usual comments teasing from such visitors.

Then one day late in the summer, while looking at a magazine at a friend's house, I happened upon a cure for my misfortune of being born with red hair and fair skin, soon splattered with those dreadful freckles. There it was — staring boldly at me from a page of ads — "Othine Freckle Cream," guaranteed to remove freckles or your money back! $1 a jar."

I carefully removed the ad from the book, hoping my friend wouldn't notice the torn page. I quickly folded the treasured find and stuffed it in my jeans pocket for closer examination later.

Nearly every day thereafter, I pulled the paper from my pocket, unfolded it, and pondered over the intriguing message, "Guaranteed to remove freckles." But the prescribed miracle was hopelessly beyond my reach, for dollars in my home with 11 children during those Depression years were few and far between. Even the bare necessities were hard to come by; but still, I remember how I continued to dream of the day when I'd be rid of those darn freckles!

School began. I still carried around the bit of paper that by now had become faded and worn — but the hope remained as vivid as ever in my mind.

With the approach of winter and still lacking the dollar needed to order the miracle cream, I formulated another possibility. I was soon dropping hints that all I wanted for Christmas was a jar of Othine, guaranteed to remove freckles. The usual boyish wishes for trucks and cars, warm mittens and boots were replaced by my one desire for finding a jar of freckles remover in my stocking on Christmas morning.

The days until Christmas crept by ever so slowly and in our family, with its numerous little ones, our hearts and minds were aglow with anticipation and excitement for the coming holiday.

The time for decorating the tree finally arrived. This annual ritual took place on Christmas Eve because of the limited space in our three-roomed house. Strings of popcorn, the usual red and green paper chains brought home from school and a few carefully preserved glass ornaments soon adorned the fragrant pinon tree that had been carried in from the nearby hills.

Then came the icicles. This was a time-consuming task for these, too, were saved and used from year to year. No matter how painstakingly they were removed from the tree and put away the Christmas before, they somehow became tangled and matted and had to be sorted and straightened one strand at a time. Anna, my oldest sister, and I were assigned to this duty as were seemed to have the most patience for such things. I didn't mind, for this helped to pass away the time on that "longest" day of the year. Our expectations grew higher and higher with each layer of icicles we hung on the tree.

Before we knew it, we were involved in the last tradition of Christmas Eve. Just before going to bed we wrote our letters to Santa Claus. Mine was short, simple and right to the point: "Dear Santa Claus. All I want for Christmas is a jar of 'Othine Freckle Cream,' guaranteed to remove freckles!"

Getting to sleep in a bed with three other brothers was difficult any time, but especially on the night before Christmas. However, drowsiness finally set in and sleep did overtake all of us. Perhaps the weight of the numerous quilts, re-covered and tied again and again, restrained our movements and helped to quiet us down. It was indeed difficult to move under such a burden.

Early the next morning, it fell my lot to build the fire in the stove to warm the house for others before they arose. This had to be accomplished without lights and no peeking under the tree or at the long row of stockings that had been carefully hung the night before. Abiding by this rule was almost more than I could bear, but I crawled back into bed true to my trust.

After much begging and coaxing, we children won Mom's and Dad's permission to get up. At about 3 a.m. we all scrambled for our socks. Those who had borrowed their sisters' long brown cotton ones were oblivious to the knots tied halfway up as they viewed the contents stuffed within.

I carefully removed my own from its place in the line, savoring each moment of anticipation. I reached inside, hardly daring to look. All the doubts I'd ever had about the existence of Santa Claus fled as my fingers clutched the only item in the sock — the treasured jar of "Othine Freckle Cream." None other than he could have fulfilled my hopes and dreams.

I don't remember getting a refund, but I do hope Santa got his money back.